THIS DAY IN
COLLECTING
HISTORY

Our thanks to the many auctions that provided information and photos for this book. Please visit their websites to learn more about them and their past, present, and future auctions.

Also, we express our sincere appreciation to Norton Publishing and *Southeastern Antiquing and Collecting Magazine* for affording us the opportunity to create *This Day in Collecting History.*

Unless otherwise noted, all auction prices realized include the buyer's premium. This is a percentage designated by the auction and added to the winning bid. The buyer's premium is an auction's price for selling an item.

THIS DAY IN
COLLECTING
HISTORY

A Year of Art, Memorabilia
& Other Treasures Sold

The value of anything is what someone is willing to pay for it
—in money, time, effort, or sacrifice.

Schiffer Publishing Ltd

4880 Lower Valley Road • Atglen, PA 19310

Michael A. McLeod and Marla K. McLeod

OTHER SCHIFFER BOOKS ON RELATED SUBJECTS:

World War II Posters, 978-0-7643-5246-1
Mai-Kai: History and Mystery of the Iconic Tiki Restaurant, 978-0-7643-5126-6
Break Out: How the Apple II Launched the PC Gaming Revolution, 978-0-7643-5322-2
The 100 Greatest Console Video Games: 1977–1987, 978-0-7643-4618-7
The World's Rarest Movie Posters, 978-0-7643-3498-6

Designed by Matthew Goodman
Credits: Timelines.ws and Wikipedia.org
All photos not credited are public domain, PD-US
Type set in Bodega Sans, Minion and Futura Std

ISBN: 978-0-7643-5341-3
Printed in China

Published by Schiffer Publishing, Ltd.
4880 Lower Valley Road
Atglen, PA 19310
Phone: (610) 593-1777; Fax: (610) 593-2002
E-mail: Info@schifferbooks.com
Web: www.schifferbooks.com

For our complete selection of fine books on this and related subjects, please visit our website at www.schifferbooks.com. You may also write for a free catalog.

Schiffer Publishing's titles are available at special discounts for bulk purchases for sales promotions or premiums. Special editions, including personalized covers, corporate imprints, and excerpts, can be created in large quantities for special needs. For more information, contact the publisher.

We are always looking for people to write books on new and related subjects. If you have an idea for a book, please contact us at proposals@schifferbooks.com.

INTRODUCTION

Joan of Arc's ring ($425,000), Luke Skywalker's X-Wing Fighter ($221,000), the Cowardly Lion's costume ($3+million), Marilyn Monroe's "Happy Birthday, Mr. President" dress ($4.8 million), the Wicked Witch of the West's hat ($208,000)—the astonishing list of pop culture, art, history, sports, movie, and celebrity items and memorabilia (and what they sold for) is recorded daily in *This Day in Collecting History*.

Every year, hundreds of auctions around the world sell these treasures, and I was fortunate enough to be notified of the highlights when I was editor of *Southeastern Antiquing and Collecting Magazine*. However for a majority of them, I have researched auctions' past sales, and frankly, much that I found is astounding. Hundreds of thousands of dollars, and often millions of dollars, are paid for paintings, sculptures, artwork, baseball cards, baseball bats, and—as you see above—costumes, rings, movie props, dresses, and hats.

But it is really about the people connected with these treasures that are the real stories. Without them and their accomplishments, there would be little value to most of these items. For instance, one of Jesse Owens' medals from the 1936 Olympics auctioned for nearly $1.5 million. He never made anything close to that amount of money during his lifetime, but that medal is a piece of history because of him.

While *This Day in Collecting History* often focuses on the treasures and the memorabilia, it is also about lauding the people who created works of art, set records for the books, and accomplished the incredible.

JANUARY

Abraham Lincoln

JANUARY 1, 1863: President Abraham Lincoln signed the Emancipation Proclamation, freeing only the slaves in the southern states that were at war with the Union. Of the 48 copies created and signed, 26 are still known to exist (freedomcenter.org).

In 2012, one copy was sold by Robert A. Siegel Auction Galleries for $2+ million. In 2010, a copy of the Emancipation Proclamation bought by Robert Kennedy in 1964 for less than $10,000 sold for $3.8 million (csmonitor.com, 6/29/12).

JANUARY 1, 1735: The birthdate of Paul Revere, patriot, silversmith, printer, engraver—and dentist? Yes, the multi-talented Revere even practiced a little dentistry at one time. In what could have been an ep-

Left: Paul Revere Right: Paul Revere's dental tools (*Photo courtesy of Otis Historical Archives National Museum of Health & Medicine*)

isode of *CSI: American Revolutionary War*, Revere was called upon to identify the body of Major General Joseph Warren, his patient. Gen. Warren was shot in the face in the Battle of Bunker (Breed's) Hill, and his body thrown into a mass grave. Months later, Revere positively identified his dental work (newenglandhistorical-society.com).

Revere's other handiwork, silver making, is not as rare as his dental work, but certain works are still very valuable. For instance, a set of five Paul Revere silver tablespoons was auctioned by Christie's in 2009 for $56,250.

JANUARY 2, 1920: Legendary science-fiction author Isaac Asimov was born—probably. Because of lack of records in Russia and conflicts in the Jewish and Julian calendars, Asimov wasn't sure of the date but chose to celebrate it on January 2.

In 2012, Asimov's 1950 novel, *I, Robot*, sold for $8,125 at Heritage Auctions. It was signed and inscribed. The novel became a movie in 2004 (IMDb.com) starring Will Smith and run-amok robots.

Left: Isaac Asimov Right: *I, Robot* (Photo courtesy of Heritage Auctions, HA.com)

JANUARY 3, 1924: The sarcophagus of King Tutankhamen was discovered by Howard Carter. It was opened later to reveal a golden coffin holding two smaller golden coffins, one within the other, all carved like King Tut's golden mask. The tomb contained three chambers and 3,500 objects (destination-yisrael.biblesearchers.com).

Carter's benefactor for his years of exploration was George Herbert, the 5th Earl of Carnarvon, the master of Highclere Castle, which was where *Downton Abbey* was filmed. He died three months after entering the tomb from an infected mosquito bite he cut while shaving, which started the myth of the Mummy's Curse.

Left: The golden mask of King Tut in the Egyptian Museum in Cairo (Photo: Bjorn Christian Torrissen) Middle: Howard Carter Right: George Herbert, Lord Carnarvon

JANUARY 4, 1643: Sir Isaac Newton celebrated his second birth date, his first being on December 25, 1642. Newton is favored with two birthdays due to two calendars being in use in his day. The Gregorian calendar, now commonly used, dated Newton's birth to January 4. The Julian calendar dated it to December 25.

Sir Isaac Newton

In 2013, Christie's auctioned Sir Isaac Newton's *Philosophiae Naturalis Principia Mathematica* of 1687, which defined the laws of motion and gravity, for $2,517,000. The January 16, 1881 edition of the *New York Times*, p. 10, reported a tooth said to have been one of Sir Isaac's was sold for £730, which some might say verifies his statement: "I can calculate the motion of heavenly bodies, but not the madness of people" (brainyquote.com).

JANUARY 5, 1922: Sir Ernest Shackleton, the intrepid British explorer of Antarctic regions, passed away from heart problems. Knighted for his bravery, Shackleton and five men once sailed in an open boat over 800+ miles of ocean and through storms to find help for his marooned crew.

In 2015, Christie's sold 15 of Shackleton's medals for $898,637 (paulfrasercollectibles.com).

Left: The polar explorers (l-r) Roald Amundsen, Shackleton, and Robert Peary (*Photo courtesy of Nasjonalbiblioteket*) Right: The launch of Shackleton's boat to find help for his marooned crew.

JANUARY 6, 1412: The birthday of Joan of Arc. On May 16, 1920, she was canonized as a saint, centuries after her death on May 30, 1431.

Joan of Arc's ring (*Photo courtesy of Timelineauctions.com*)

In February 2016, the Puy du Fou Foundation purchased Joan of Arc's silver-gilt devotional ring for almost $425,000 at an auction in England and brought it home to France. Facetted faces on the ring show "I" and "IHS" for "Jesus" and "M" and "MAR" for "Maria" (timelineauctions.com).

JANUARY 6, 2016: A Roosevelt dime imprint that was accidentally struck into a sixpenny nail hammered for $42,300 at Heritage Auctions. Even in that state, the dime portion was graded highly at MS65—no report of what the rest of the nail was graded.

Other printing errors have brought quite a few bucks. For instance, a Del Monte banana sticker that somehow became stuck to the currency paper of a $20 bill before it was printed made $25,300 at Heritage Auctions in 2006.

Above The Del Monte Note (*Photo courtesy of Heritage Auctions, HA.com*) Top: The dime-imprinted nail (*Photo courtesy of Heritage Auctions, HA.com*)

JANUARY 7, 1714: The first patent for a typewriter was issued to Henry Mill. In 2012, *Guinness World Records* listed Ian Fleming's gold-plated Royal Quiet Deluxe typewriter as the most expensive at $90,309. The diligent folks at Guinness must have missed author Cormac McCarthy's Olivetti typewriter selling for $254,500 in 2009 at Christie's. McCormack typed all his novels on his Olivetti, including *No Country For Old Men, The Orchard Keeper,* and *All the Pretty Horses.*

A golden Royal Quiet Deluxe typewriter like Ian Fleming's

JANUARY 7, 2016: A real dime, an 1894-S Barber Dime, Branch Mint PR66, spiked at $1,997,500 at Heritage Auctions. Because of the Panic of 1893 and little demand for dimes at the time, only 24 of these coins were struck at the San Francisco Mint. Only eight or nine are known to exist.

1894-S Barber Dime *(Photo courtesy of Heritage Auctions, HA.com)*

JANUARY 8, 1935: The King was born. Elvis Presley made Tupelo, Mississippi, and banana, peanut butter, and bacon sandwiches famous.

Fans and collectors still go crazy for the King. So much so that Elvis earned about $55 million during 2013–2014 (forbes.com, 10/15/14), even though he passed away on Aug. 16, 1977. Someone paid $115,000 for a lock of his hair (historychannel.com, 11/16/02). In 2014, Bonham's sold "The ex-King of Rock 'n Roll Elvis Presley's 1963 Rolls-Royce Phantom V Touring Limousine" for $396,000.

Elvis in *Jailhouse Rock*

JANUARY 9, 1906: The trademark for Campbell's Soup was registered.

In 2010, Andy Warhol's *Big Campbell's Soup Can with Can Opener (Vegetable)*, signed and dated "Andy Warhol 62" and measuring 72 x 52 inches, auctioned for $23,882,500 at Christie's. Other paintings from his Campbell's Soup Can series have also sold for millions. Warhol once said he ate Campbell's Soup every day for two decades (warhol.org).

Andy Warhol

JANUARY 10, 1776: Thomas Paine published *Common Sense* and sold more than 500,000 copies of it, making him a pretty penny while helping to spark the American Revolution. Despite the huge amount printed, *Common Sense* still has collectible gravitas—one copy auctioned in 2013 for $545,000 at Sotheby's. Thomas Paine was also born this month on January 29, 1737.

Thomas Paine

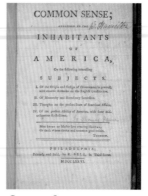

Common Sense

JANUARY 10, 2014: The highest price for a currency bill was paid at auction this day for the 1890 Small Seal Grand Watermelon—$3,290,000 at Heritage Auctions.

Grand Watermelon (*Photos courtesy of Heritage Auctions, HA.com*)

The reverse of the Watermelon

This $1,000 bill is the rarest currency note, and it received its nickname from the three large zeroes on the back which look like watermelons.

JANUARY 11, 1964:

The Surgeon General declared cigarette smoking caused cancer in men and "probably" in women (cdc. gov). Ironically, German doctors recognized the detrimental effects of smoking in the 1930s, and Hitler's government started the first anti-smoking advertising campaign.

In 2010, a Home Run cigar tin with an image of baseball players on the field made by Federal Tin Co. went for $18,400 at Morphy Auctions.

Home Run cigar tin (*Photo courtesy of Morphy Auctions*)

According to a recent Nationwide survey:

MORE DOCTORS SMOKE CAMELS THAN ANY OTHER CIGARETTE

This 1946 ad declares, "More Doctors Smoke Camels . . ." (*Photo: tobacco. stanford.edu, "Stanford Research into the Impact of Tobacco Advertising"*)

JANUARY 12, 1966: *Batman* starring Adam West and Burt Ward roared out of the Batcave and into history; the show lasted three seasons (IMDb.com).

The original Batmobile (*Photo courtesy of Jennifer Graylock/ Ford Motor Company*)

Burt Ward and Adam West

(Continued on the next page.)

Batmobile #1, owned and created by Chuck Barris with a 1955 Lincoln Futura, roared off for $4,620,000 at Barrett-Jackson Auctions in 2013. Barris created three other Batmobiles out of fiberglass; the original was steel (1966batmobile.com).

JANUARY 13, 1930: The first appearance of Mickey Mouse in a comic strip. Original art for a January 29, 1930 Mickey Mouse Daily #15 comic strip by Ub Iwerks and Win Smith sold for $74,750 in 2006 at Heritage Auctions.

Mickey Mouse before the movies (*Photo courtesy of Heritage Auctions, HA.com*)

JANUARY 14, 1954: Joe DiMaggio married Marilyn Monroe. She filed for divorce less than a year later.

The platinum and diamond wedding ring Joe gave Marilyn auctioned for $504,000 at Profiles in History in 2011. Before that, a higher bid at Christie's in 1999 sent it off for $772,500.

Marilyn and Joe

JANUARY 15, 1929: Martin Luther King, Jr. was born in Atlanta. He received the Nobel Peace Prize in 1964.

A first edition of Rev. Dr. Martin Luther King, Jr.'s book, *Stride Toward Freedom*, inscribed to Chief Justice Earl Warren in 1959, went for $49,335 at Hake's Americana in 2015.

Martin Luther King, Jr.'s *Stride Toward Freedom*
(*Photo courtesy of Hakes.com*)

JANUARY 16, 1910: Birthday cake for pitching legend and Hall of Famer Jay Hanna "Dizzy" Dean. With 1,163 strikeouts and a win-loss record of 150–83, he was an All-Star four times, MLB Strikeout Leader four times, and a World Series Champion.

A 1936 Dizzy Dean St. Louis Cardinal's jersey brought $103,500 at Robert Edward Auctions in 2004.

Dizzy said: "Son, what kind of pitch would you like to miss?" and "Anybody who's ever had the privilege of seeing me play knows that I am the greatest pitcher in the world" (dizzydean.com).

This 1930s Dizzy Dean photo sold for $382.40 in 2015 at Heritage Auctions. *(Photo courtesy of Heritage Auctions, HA. com)*

JANUARY 17, 1706: Born this day in Boston was Benjamin Franklin. The talented inventor, author, and statesman made this no-nonsense comment: "He that is good for making excuses is seldom good for anything else" (brainyquote.com).

A Benjamin Franklin-signed interest certificate as President of Pennsylvania and dated 19 October 1785 sold for $15,436 at Nate D. Sanders Auctions in 2013.

JANUARY 17, 1942: Muhammad (Cassius Clay) Ali shared the same day of birth with Ben Franklin. From saying, "I am the greatest!" to "Service to others is the rent

Ali's and Liston's signed gloves *(Photo courtesy of Heritage Auctions, HA.com)*

(Continued on the next page.)

I pay for my room here on earth," Muhammad Ali was a great philanthropist, as well as perhaps the greatest boxer ever.

The boxing gloves worn by him and Sonny Liston in their May of 1965 rematch reaped $956,000 at Heritage Auctions in 2015. Both sets of gloves were confiscated by the boxing commissioner after Ali knocked down Liston with supposedly a "phantom punch." Some said Ali did not connect. Liston was counted out before he got up.

JANUARY 18, 1904: British actor Archibald Alexander Leach was born, otherwise known to the world as Cary Grant. Early in his life, he acted in the theater and was an acrobat, juggler, and stilt walker. *North By Northwest, Father Goose, That Touch of Mink, Arsenic and Old Lace*—Grant had 76 screen credits during his career.

In 2011, the sport coat he wore in *To Catch A Thief* was sold for $18,450 by Profiles in History.

Cary Grant

JANUARY 19: A big day for birthdays: Robert E. Lee, 1807; Edgar Allan Poe, 1809; and Paul Cézanne, 1839.

Cezanne's *The Card Players* fetched about $259 million in a private sale to Qatar in 2012 (vanityfair.com, 2/12/12). Cézanne died in 1906 from pneumonia, a few days after working in the rain for two hours.

Cezanne's *The Card Players*

Paul Cezanne

JANUARY 20, 1896: Comedian George Burns was born (as Nathan Birnbaum)—to perform in vaudeville, on the radio, on TV, in movies, and today on the Internet.

After his death at age 100, an estate sale of his personal effects reached $365,000 at Sotheby's in 1996. Items sold included: a Grandma Moses painting, $13,000+; two pairs of his wife Gracie Allen's cat eye glasses, $1,600; an 18th century commode, $11,000; and diamond cuff links with Burns' initials purchased by Jerry Seinfeld for $12,650 (articles.latimes.com, 10/11/96).

George Burns

George Burns once said: "Happiness is having a large, loving, caring, close-knit family. . . in another city" (brainyquote.com).

JANUARY 21, 1793: King Louis XVI of France was guillotined on this day after the French Revolution. Queen Marie Antoinette followed him in October. In addition to supporting the colonists in the American Revolution— for whom Louisville, Kentucky, is named— Louis XVI is remembered for the style of furniture that bears his name. It waned in popularity after his execution.

A Louis XVI secretary, once owned by Alphonse de Rothschild, was auctioned at Sotheby's for $2,090,000 in 1986.

King Louis XVI in 1775

JANUARY 22, 1901: Queen Victoria of England passed away. She was the longest reigning monarch of England for 63 years until she was surpassed by Queen Elizabeth II in September 2015.

From furniture to paperweights, the Victorian Age gave the world many categories of collectibles. A pair of silver Victorian asparagus tongs served up about $421 (£288) in 2007 at Bonhams.

Queen Victoria, 1843

JANUARY 22, 2016: The Wiltshire and Swindon History Centre reported on this day on its website (www.wiltshire.gov.uk) that a badger dug up a haul of archaeological artifacts: shards from a pottery funeral urn, a serrated copper saw blade, an archer's wrist guard, stones for straightening arrow shafts, and a copper chisel blade. A passerby found them about five miles from Stonehenge in May 2014.

The artifacts dated to the Bronze Age, about 2200–2000 B.C., which was in the early days of Stonehenge (bbc.com, 2/9/16). They were taken to the Wiltshire and Swindon History Centre for conservation.

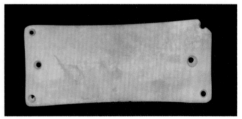

The badger-dug copper saw (*Photos courtesy of the Wiltshire Council CMAS*)

The Bronze Age wristguard

JANUARY 23, 1737: John Hancock was born in Massachusetts and became the first signer of the Declaration of Independence while serving as President of the Second Continental Congress. John Hancock did not start an insurance company.

Even though his name has become generic for all signatures, his is valuable. His autograph on a document while governor of Massachusetts, dated 1784, sold for $2,000 at Christie's in 2010.

John Hancock

JANUARY 24, 1965: Winston Churchill died at the age of 90.

The Victory watch presented to him after WWII secured $751,556 (£485,000) in 2015 at Sotheby's.

Winston Churchill's watch (*Photos courtesy of Sotheby's*)

JANUARY 24, 2013: A 1794 Flowing Hair silver dollar auctioned for $10 million, the most paid for a coin to date. It is believed to be the first metal coin struck in the US. Of all the 1794 dollars, it is the only to have a silver plug added to the coin blank before minting to bring it to standard weight (coinworld.com, 12/31/14).

The Flowing Hair dollar (*Photos courtesy of Stack's Bowers Gallery*)

The coin's reverse

JANUARY 25, 1936: Voting for the first five inductees to the Baseball Hall of Fame ended with the election of: Ty Cobb, Walter Johnson, Christy Mathewson, Babe Ruth, and Honus Wagner (history.com/this-day-in-history).

A 1915 Cracker Jack, Walter Johnson #57 card rated PSA mint 9 auctioned for $101,575 at Heritage Auctions in 2016. The auction also listed this quote from Ty Cobb about Johnson: "The first time I faced him, I watched him take that easy windup. . . . And then something went past me that made me flinch. The thing just hissed with danger. We couldn't touch him. Every one of us knew we'd met the most powerful arm ever turned loose in a ballpark."

"The Big Train" Walter Johnson's Cracker Jack card (*Photo courtesy of Heritage Auctions, HA.com*)

JANUARY 25, 1947: Mobster Al Capone died on this day at 48 of pneumonia and heart attack.

In 2011, Christie's gave up Capone's nickel-plated Colt .38 caliber revolver for $109,080.

JANUARY 26, 2014: Keno Auctions sold a 1775 letter entitled, "The Twelve United Colonies, by their Delegates in Congress, to the Inhabitants of Great Britain," primarily written by Robert R. Livingston, who assisted in drafting the Declaration of Independence. It went for $912,500. The document was found among old bills in a drawer in the attic of the Morris-Jumel Mansion and Museum in Manhattan.

Robert R. Livingston

JANUARY 26, 1892: The first African-American aviator, Bessie Coleman, was born. A sharecropper's daughter, she learned French to go to France and take flying lessons—no flying school in America would accept her.

In 1995, the Post Office issued a Bessie Coleman 32¢ stamp, and in 2006 Bessie was inducted into the National Aviation Hall of Fame.

Bessie Coleman

JANUARY 27: The birthdays of Charles Lutwidge Dodgson, better known as Lewis Carroll, 1832, in England, and Wolfgang Amadeus Mozart, 1756, in Austria. A prolific author and mathematician, Carroll also invented a double-sided adhesive tape and the nyctograph for writing in the dark.

His books about Alice and Wonderland made him world-famous and rich. His personal copy of *Alice's Adventures in Wonderland*, marked in purple ink and with ten original drawings by illustrator John Tenniel (including one of the Cheshire Cat), sold for $1,542,500 in 1998 at Christie's; it is one of twenty-two original 1865 editions known to exist.

Lewis Carroll

JANUARY 28, 2012: Pancho Villa's last saddle rode off for $750,000 from High Noon Western Americana. Crafted with silver-wrapped threads, Villa's widow gave it to movie director Howard Hawks as a present for his film, *Viva Villa* (1934), which portrayed her revolutionary and outlaw husband favorably.

In 1916, Villa and his men attacked Columbus, NM, and the 13th Cavalry

[Continued on the next page.]

Pancho Villa

Pancho Villa's saddle (*Photos courtesy of High Noon Western Americana*)

Regiment there, killing at least fifteen people and burning the town. He lost 80 of his men. Villa was assassinated in 1923 by a group of his countrymen while being driven in his 1915 Dodge Touring car.

JANUARY 29, 1945: Actor, screenwriter, and producer Tom Selleck was born. Famous for his *Magnum, P.I.* and *Blue Bloods* TV series (IMDb. com), he also starred in *Quigley Down Under*, a cowboy movie set in Australia. His Shiloh Sharps Hartford rifle, one of three created for the movie and the one he took home, sold for $69,000 at James D. Julia Auctions in 2008.

Tom Selleck

Paul Newman and Joanne Woodward

JANUARY 29, 1958: The stars aligned with the marriage this day of Paul Newman and Joanne Woodward. Both won an Oscar during their careers: Woodward for Best Actress in *The Three Faces of Eve* (1957) and Newman for *The Color of Money* (1986). Newman's success in movies like *Butch Cassidy and The Sundance Kid*, *The Sting*, and *Cool Hand Luke* probably assisted in his becoming a great collector of cars. A 2002 Corvette he won his last race in before passing away in 2008 gaveled for $275,000 at RM Auctions in 2012 (blog.wsj.com, 3/11/12).

Paul Newman and A.E. Hotchner founded Newman's Own food company (popcorn, pasta sauce, salad dressing, salsa, frozen pizza, frozen dinners, and drinks) that donates all after-tax profits to Newman's Own Foundation, which gives the money to charities—more than $460 million to date (newmansownfoundation.org). Funds also support Hole in the Wall camps worldwide (which Paul Newman helped create) for children with life-threatening illnesses.

JANUARY 29, 1959: Disney released *Sleeping Beauty*. Cels from the movie can sell in the five-figure and six-figure range. A *Sleeping Beauty* hand-painted background cel set-up by Eyvind Earl showing fairies in the royal throne room brought $35,850 in 2009 at Heritage Auctions.

The *Sleeping Beauty* background cel (*Photo courtesy of Heritage Auctions, HA.com*)

JANUARY 30, 1882: Franklin Delano Roosevelt was born in New York State. The only four-term president, Roosevelt died in office after a stroke.

The beaver fur top hat he wore for his first presidential inauguration on March 4, 1933 sold for $46,875 at RR Auction in 2014.

FDR, 1933

JANUARY 31, 1919: Jackie Robinson was born in the little town of Cairo, Georgia, destined to break the color barrier in American baseball. His skills earned him a spot in the Baseball Hall of Fame in 1962. He played nine years for the Brooklyn Dodgers and retired with a .311 batting average, 137 home runs, and 1,518 hits.

A 1952 Topps Jackie Robinson #312 card rated PSA NM-MT 8 hit $35,850 at Heritage Auctions in 2016.

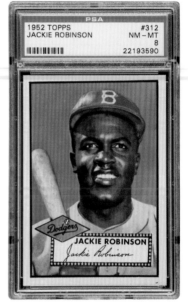

Jackie Robinson's card (*Photo courtesy of Heritage Auctions, HA.com*)

FEBRUARY

FEBRUARY 1, 1901: Frankly, Scarlett, it's my birthday. Clark (his real name) Gable earned $120,000 while working seventy-one days filming *Gone With The Wind*. Vivien Leigh earned $25,000 for working 125 days (IMDb.com)—about $422,000 in today's money.

Her Oscar for Best Actress in *Gone With The Wind* auctioned for $563,500 at Sotheby's in 1993 (variety.com, 12/15/93). Gable's Best Actor Oscar for *It Happened One Night* (his only Oscar) hit $607,500 in 1996 at Christie's. Michael Jackson bought David O. Selznick's Academy Award for

Clark Gable

Best Picture for *Gone With The Wind* for $1.54 million in 1999 at Sotheby's (hollywoodreporter.com, 2/24/16).

FEBRUARY 2, 1996: Actor, singer, dancer Gene Kelly passed away. He performed the famous "Singin' in the Rain" song and dance routine in the movie while extremely ill and wet. He did it in one take (IMDb.com).

The gray wool suit he wore in that number sold for $106,250 at Heritage Auctions in 2013.

Co-star Donald O'Connor's trick of running up a

Gene Kelly

Donald O'Connor

Far Right: The "Singin' in the Rain" suit
(*Photo courtesy of Heritage Auctions, HA.com*)

wall and doing a somersault back onto his feet sent him to bed for three days. He was a four-pack-a-day smoker then, and he landed on a concrete floor all day during shooting. After recovering, he had to do it all over again because the original film was damaged (IMDb.com).

FEBRUARY 2, 1969: William Henry Pratt died at the age of 81. Born in London, he played fearsome characters under the stage name of "Boris Karloff." Frankenstein, the Mummy, Dr. Fu Manchu, and the voice of the Grinch and the narrator in *How The Grinch Stole Christmas*—Karloff was a classic.

Boris Karloff

Frankenstein movie posters sell in the range of a few hundred dollars to a few hundred thousand dollars. A 41 x 78.5-inch, three sheet Style C *Frankenstein* (1931) poster hit a frightening $358,500 in 2015. *A Bride of Frankenstein* one sheet Style D poster auctioned in 2007 for $334,600—same money for *The Black Cat* (1934) in 2009, a one sheet Style B. Karloff's costume from *The Black Cat* sold for $89,625 in 2009. All at Heritage Auctions and all Boris Karloff. One more, *The Mummy* (1932) starring Boris Karloff auctioned for $453,500 at Sotheby's (nytimes. com, 4/17/99).

Left: (Photo courtesy of Heritage Auctions, HA.com) Right: The Black Cat costume (Photo courtesy of Heritage Auctions, HA.com)

FEBRUARY 3, 1468: Johannes Gutenberg passed away.

A Gutenberg Bible hammered for $5.4 million in 1987 at Christie's (nyt.com, 10/23/87). Printed in the 1450s, the British Library records that Gutenberg printed 180 bibles, and forty-eight are still in existence, not all being complete (bl.uk). A single leaf from a Gutenberg Bible sold for $56,250 at Christie's in 2012.

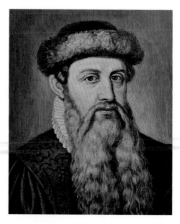

Left: A Gutenberg Bible in the New York Public Library (*Photo courtesy of NYC Wanderer Kevin Eng*)
Right: Johannes Gutenberg

FEBRUARY 4, 1902: Charles Lindbergh was born to fly. A letter and envelope he carried on the first solo flight across the Atlantic to Paris on May 20-21, 1927 brought $110,000 in 2001, and another letter landed at $155,000 in 1999, both at Robert Siegel Auction Galleries.

Lindbergh carried no parachute with him on that flight, figuring there was no need for one if he did not make it (charleslindbergh.com). He lived until 1974.

Charles Lindbergh with the *Spirit of St. Louis*, 1927

FEBRUARY 4, 1913: The birthday of "The First Lady of Civil Rights" Rosa Parks in Tuskegee, Alabama. Nine years after her passing in 2005, her personal effects (including her Presidential Medal of Freedom and Congressional Gold Medal) were sold by Guernsey's for $4.5 million (usatoday.com, 9-15-14).

Rosa Parks

FEBRUARY 5, 1934: Hank Aaron was born in Mobile, Alabama. As a youth, he practiced slugging homers by hitting bottle caps with a broomstick. His home run record of 755 bested Babe Ruth's 714.

A Hank Aaron game-worn jersey from 1969 went for $50,126.99 in 2013 at Lelands.com.

Hank Aaron at his Hall of Fame induction in 1982 (*Photo courtesy of Magnus Manske*)

FEBRUARY 6, 1895: Birth of the Bambino, the Sultan of Swat, the Babe, George Herman Ruth, Jr. When the Babe tried to trademark his own candy called Ruth's Home Run, the Curtiss Candy Company filed suit saying he was infringing on their copyright of the "Baby Ruth" name. The company declared it named the candy after President Grover Cleveland's daughter Ruth—even though she'd died years before, and Cleveland had been out of office for twenty-nine years. Yet, the court ruled in favor of Curtiss, putting the Babe out of the candy business.

Ruth's Home Run candy (*Photo courtesy of Robert Edward Auctions*)

[Continued on the next page.]

Ruth's Home Run candy cards

④ "BABE" RUTH
The Popular Bambino eating his Home Run Candy. His Candy Helped Him.

⑤ "BABE" RUTH
A favorite with the Kiddies
Babe Ruth's Own Candy

Now, Ruth's Home Run candy wrappers are relatively rare. Robert Edward Auctions sold a wrapper in 2008 for $1,750. And what would Babe Ruth candy be without a baseball card? Six cards were produced, and they promised kids a free Babe Ruth-signed ball for collecting all and sending them in (number5typecollection.com), which is why few wrappers are left today. A pair with scenes from the movie, *Babe Comes Home,* sold for $439 at SCP Auctions.

FEBRUARY 7: Authors Charles Dickens, 1812, and Laura Ingalls Wilder, 1867, share this birthday. Dickens worked as a child laborer like his Oliver Twist character. This experience paid off in his lifetime in book sales, and Dickens continues to sell today. An autographed first edition of *Oliver Twist* garnered $229,000 in 2008 at Christie's.

Charles Dickens

Laura Ingalls Wilder

Laura Ingalls Wilder's eight *Little House on the Prairie* books and seventeen other works made her an American celebrity, and the TV show starring Melissa Gilbert and Michael Landon that ran for nine years didn't hurt either.

A Laura Ingalls Wilder handwritten, autographed letter to a fan gaveled at Bonhams in 2012 for $1,375.

FEBRUARY 8: Born this
day were James Dean in
Marion, Indiana, 1931,
and Jules Verne in Nantes,
France, 1828. The *East
of Eden*, *Rebel Without
A Cause*, and *Giant* star
James Dean was also an
artist. His painting, *The
Road To Happiness*, sold
for $8,962.50 in 2006 at
Heritage Auctions. His
autograph is worth thou-
sands due to his tragic
death at the age of twen-
ty-four (paulfrasercollectibles.com).

The Road to Happiness (Photo
courtesy of Heritage Auctions,
HA.com)

Jules Verne

James Dean

In 2015, Swann Galleries auctioned a first edition of
Jules Verne's *From the Earth to the Moon* for $22,500. A
later edition (published in 1918) sold in 2013 at Heritage
Auctions for $7,500, and it was signed by eleven Apollo
astronauts, including: Walt Cunningham (Apollo 7), Frank
Borman (Apollo 8), Gene Cernan (Apollo 10 and 17), and Buzz Aldrin (Apollo 11).

FEBRUARY 9, 1971: Leroy Robert "Satchel" Paige was nominated for the Baseball
Hall of Fame; he was inducted in August of 1971 (history.com). One of his two Hall
of Fame rings made $25,000 in 2015 at Lelands, which reported that the other ring
was sold previously by his family for $259,642 at SCP Auctions in 2014.

LEROY "Satchell" PAIGE

Satchel Paige

Satchel's 1971 Hall of Fame ring
(Photos courtesy of Lelands.com)

FEBRUARY 10, 2005: Playwright Arthur Miller passed away. His second wife was Marilyn Monroe, and several of his love letters to her sold individually at Julien's in 2014, the highest bringing $43,750.

Miller authored *Death of a Salesman* (which won a Pulitzer Prize for Drama in 1949), *The Crucible,* and other plays. He also wrote the script for the movie, *The Misfits,* starring Clark Gable and his wife, Marilyn Monroe.

Arthur Miller

FEBRUARY 11, 1847: Thomas Edison was born, and he is credited with more than 1,000 US patents and an additional 1,000+ foreign patents. Many of his inventions changed the world, including the phonograph, movie camera, and stock ticker.

An Edison Electric Pen realized $22,225 at Christie's in 2002. The electric pen was a handheld device that rapidly punched holes in paper to make a stencil for duplicating forms—sort of a very early mimeograph or copier.

Thomas Edison, 1915

FEBRUARY 12, 1809: Abraham Lincoln was born in Kentucky. In January 2015, the 302-lot Dow Collection of Lincoln memorabilia topped out at $803,889 at Heritage Auctions, including: a clip of President Lincoln's hair taken by the surgeon attending him, $25,000; a letter signed by Lincoln authorizing

Admittance card to Lincoln's funeral (*Photo courtesy of Heritage Auctions, HA.com*)

the exchange of Robert E. Lee's son who was a prisoner of war, $27,500; a piece of blood-stained linen from President Lincoln's deathbed, $6,000; John Wilkes Booth's arrest warrant, $21,250; a White House funeral admittance card, $11,875; and photographs, diaries, and letters.

FEBRUARY 13, 1891: Birthday of Grant Wood, the creator of the iconic and often lampooned *American Gothic*. In 2016, the Carnegie-Stout Public Library in Dubuque, Iowa, turned down an offer of $6 million to buy a painting in its collection, *The Appraisal*, by Grant Wood (omaha.com, 1/25/16).

Grant Wood's self-portrait

Grant Wood's *The Appraisal*

American Gothic

FEBRUARY 14, 1894: Jack Benny was born in Chicago. He once said, "I don't deserve this award, but I have arthritis, and I don't deserve that either."

A Jack Benny-signed violin inscribed, "To Ray, Best wishes, Jack Benny," auctioned for $15,360 at Julien's Live in 2010.

Jack Benny, 1971

FEBRUARY 15, 1564: Birthday of Galileo Galilei in Pisa, Italy (according to the Julian calendar). Galileo's 1610 *Sidereus Nuncius* (The Starry Messenger) describing his observations by telescope of craters on the moon, four moons of Jupiter, and stars unseen without a telescope auctioned for $662,500 in 2010 at Christie's.

Two years later, Kiko Auctioneers sold the shuttlecraft *Galileo* from the original *Star Trek* series for $70,150 (giantfreakinrobot.com, 6/30/12). The boxy spaceship was weatherworn and in desperate need of restoration.

Galileo

FEBRUARY 16, 1972: Wilt Chamberlain scored his 30,000th point, the first to do so. Can you name the four other NBA players who have also scored 30,000 points so far?

On March 2, 1962, seven-foot-one-inch tall "Wilt the Stilt" was the first—and only—player to score one hundred points in an NBA game; Wilt's Philadelphia Warriors scored 169 to the New York Knicks' 147. Chamberlain's one hundred-point ball had a high bid of $551,844 in 2000 at Lelands—but the sale was withdrawn when it was claimed this was not the actual one hundred-point ball. After Wilt's shot, fourteen-year-old Kerry Ryan congratulated him and then ran off with the ball. After the statute of limitations ran out, the ball was put up for auction.

But cue the replay—the referee said he pulled the

Wilt Chamberlain

one hundred-point ball from the game and gave Wilt a different one for the last few seconds, which some say was Ryan's ball. Consequently, that ball later sold for only $67,791 at Lelands. Chamberlain held no grudge against Ryan for taking the ball (espn.go.com, 7/22/02).

No other NBA players have scored one hundred points in a game—but an incredible twenty-seven high school players have reached that pinnacle, including six girls and twenty-one boys (www.complex.com, 4/7/15).

Who has scored 30,000 points along with Wilt Chamberlain? Kareem Abdul Jabbar, Kobe Bryant, Karl Malone, and Michael Jordan (www.allaboutbasketball.us).

FEBRUARY 17, 1963: Michael Jordan was born this day in Brooklyn, New York. In 2014, he made more money from sports shoes—$100 million—than he made in his entire fifteen years of contracts in the NBA—$94 million (cbssports.com, 9/14/15). In 2015, SCP Auctions sold a pair of Michael Jordan's Nike Air Ships, signed and game-worn in 1984, for $71,553. Topping that, Upper Deck paid $1 million in 1999 for the hardwood floor in Salt Lake City's Delta Center where MJ won his last championship (complex.com, 2/17/13).

Michael Jordan

FEBRUARY 18, 1898: The racing legend who would eventually put fourteen wins at Le Mans under his seatbelt, Enzo Ferrari, was born in Italy. The first Ferrari automobile with the famous horse badge appeared in 1947, and since then classics have finished at: $38.1 million for a 1962 Ferrari 250 GTO; $27.5 million for a 1967 Ferrari 275 GTB/4 NART Spider; $26.4 million for a 1964 Ferrari 275 GTB/C Speciale; $18.4 million for a 1961 Ferrari 250 GT SWB California Spider; and $18.3 million for a 1954 Ferrari 375 Plus (hagerty.com, 12/9/15).

Enzo Ferrari

A 1962 Ferrari 250 GTO (*Photo courtesy of Sfoskett*)

FEBRUARY 18, 2016: Spider-Man arrived in *Amazing Fantasy #15* in 1962. A 9.4 rated, near-mint copy of it hammered this day at Heritage Auctions for $454,100.

The first appearance of Spider-Man (*Photo courtesy of Heritage Auctions, HA.com*)

FEBRUARY 19, 1473: Nicolaus Copernicus was born in Poland and changed the world by revealing it revolved around the sun. His 1543 treatise explaining this totally new concept, *De Revolutionibus Orbium Coelestium, Libri V*, sold for $2,210,500 in 2008 at Christie's.

Nicolaus Copernicus

FEBRUARY 20, 1902: The birthday of Ansel Adams, the black-and-white photographer extraordinaire. In addition to landscapes, Adams also took photos of Japanese in US internment camps during WWII. His *Moonrise, Hernandez, New Mexico* (1948), signed and printed in 1948, was auctioned for $609,600 in 2006. In 2015, this photo, probably printed between 1963 and 1970, sold for $56,250, both at Sotheby's.

Ansel Adams

FEBRUARY 20, 1895: Former slave, abolitionist, equal rights advocate, author, and legendary orator Frederick Douglass passed away this day. He wrote three autobiographies: *Narrative of the Life of Frederick Douglass, An American Slave, My Bondage and My Freedom,* and *Life and Times of Frederick Douglass.*

In 2010, an ambrotype (glass) quarter plate portrait of him from the 1870s made $20,000 at Jackson's in Cedar Falls, Iowa.

The Frederick Douglass ambrotype
(*Photo courtesy of Jackson's*)

FEBRUARY 21, 1994: CIA agent Aldrich Ames was arrested for spying as a double agent for the Soviet Union for six years. His treason resulted in the deaths of many people. He was sentenced to life without parole. In 2015, 170+ letters Ames wrote from prison went for $9,000 at Lion Heart Autographs (livescience.com, 10/5/15).

FEBRUARY 22, 1732: George Washington, "The Father of Our Country," was born. Among the top items in the Mount Vernon collection are: Washington's dress sword; his round presidential chair

The key to the Bastille (*Photo courtesy of George Washington's Mount Vernon*)

George Washington's tomb at Mount Vernon

that swiveled; the key to the Bastille given to him by the Marquis de Lafayette who commanded the Paris National Guard when the prison was taken; and one of Washington's many sets of dentures. The set in the collection was made of human, cow, and horse teeth and elephant ivory (mountvernon.org).

FEBRUARY 23, 1685: Hallelujah! George Frideric Handel was born (on the Julian calendar; March 5 on today's Gregorian calendar). Composer of forty-two operas and twenty-nine oratorios, including the heavenly *Messiah*, Handel was also an art collector, amassing at least eighty paintings and prints—that were mostly auctioned off after his death on April 14, 1759 because he had no heirs.

An ad for the auction of Handel's art

George Frideric Handel

FEBRUARY 24, 2014: Actor, writer, director, and ghostbuster Harold Ramis went to the Great Beyond. He acted in and wrote the scripts for the *Ghostbusters* movies and *Stripes*, and he wrote and directed *Caddyshack*, *Groundhog Day*, *National Lampoon's Vacation*, and other films. One of three 1959 Cadillac Custom Ghostbusters cars made for the movies sold for $88,000 at Barrett-Jackson in 2010.

Ghostbusters poster, $262.90 in 2011 at Heritage Auctions (*Photo courtesy of Heritage Auctions, HA.com*)

FEBRUARY 25, 1841: The birth of Pierre-Auguste Renoir in Limoges, France. As a young man, Renoir worked in a porcelain factory as a design painter (metmuseum.org). Renoir's *Bal du moulin de la Galette* auctioned for $78.1 million at Sotheby's in 1990 (a *galette* is a flat, round, crusty cake).

Bal du moulin de la Galette

Pierre Renoir, c. 1910

FEBRUARY 25, 1836: Samuel Colt received a patent for a pistol with a revolving cylinder. However, one of the famous pistols bearing his name, the Colt .45 Single Action Army, or "Peacemaker," was not created until ten years after his death in 1862 (history.com, 7/18/14). An 1836 Colt .36 caliber revolver, cased with equipment, hit $977,500 in 2011 at Heritage Auctions. It had ivory grips, a 9-inch barrel, and was engraved with a stagecoach holdup scene on the cylinder.

Samuel Colt

The 1836 Colt revolver (*Photo courtesy of Heritage Auctions, HA.com*)

FEBRUARY 26, 1802: Birthday of the author of *Les Miserables* and *The Hunchback of Notre Dame*, Victor Hugo. In 2012, The Hugo Collection of the family's books, his artwork (yes, he was an artist, too), photos, and other items secured $4.3 million at Christie's (artnews.com, 5/8/12).

Victor Hugo

FEBRUARY 26, 1846: William Frederick "Buffalo Bill" Cody was born. As a scout for the US Army, Cody fought in more than a dozen battles and won the Medal of Honor for bravery. He excelled

Cody's revolver (*Photo courtesy of Heritage Auctions, HA.com*)

Buffalo Bill Cody

as a hunter, horseman, scout, and showman. Buffalo Bill's Wild West and Congress of Rough Riders of the World toured the US and Europe and featured Sitting Bull and Annie Oakley. American Indians, Turks, Arabs, Mongols, and gauchos in the show amazed crowds with their costumes, horsemanship, and marksmanship.

In 2012, Buffalo Bill Cody's Remington New Model Army .44 percussion revolver and accompanying letters, photos, and ephemera gaveled for $239,000 at Heritage Auctions.

FEBRUARY 27: Three notables born this day were: Elizabeth Taylor, 1932; John Steinbeck, 1902; and Henry Wadsworth Longfellow, 1807. In 2011, the Collection of Elizabeth Taylor—1,778 lots of jewelry, fashion, art, and film memorabilia—triumphed with an incredible $115,932,000 at Christie's. The top item was the 16th century La Peregrina pearl (202.24 grains, equal to 50+ carats) necklace with diamonds and rubies at $11.8 million.

Elizabeth Taylor, 1953

John Steinbeck

Longfellow in 1868

[Continued on the next page.]

Author of more than two dozen novels, including *The Grapes of Wrath*, *Of Mice and Men*, and *East of Eden*, an auction of John Steinbeck's letters, manuscripts, photos, and other items hammered for $73,950 in 2010 at Bloomsbury Auctions (artdaily.com).

An extremely popular poet in his day, Longfellow authored *The Song of Hiawatha* and "The Village Blacksmith" ("Under a spreading chestnut tree, The village smithy stands . . ."). Two pages of Longfellow's working manuscript translation of Dante's *Inferno* from *The Divine Comedy* brought $10,455 at Skinners in 2015.

FEBRUARY 28, 1983: "Goodbye, Farewell and Amen," the last episode of *M*A*S*H* aired in a two-and-one-half-hour movie. It was the 256th episode of the TV comedy series about doctors in the Korean War. The show premiered in 1972 and lasted for eleven seasons; it still airs today in syndication. It starred Alan "Hawkeye" Alda, Wayne "Trapper" Rogers, Loretta "Hot Lips" Swit, Harry "Col. Potter" Morgan, McLean "Lt. Col. Henry Blake" Stevenson, Jamie "Klinger" Farr, Mike "B.J. Hunnicut" Farrell, David Ogden "Charles" Stiers, Larry "Major Burns" Linville, William "Father Mulcahy" Christopher, and Gary "Radar" Burghoff (IMDb.com).

The cast, clockwise from Loretta Swit: Larry Linville, Wayne Rogers, Gary Burghoff, McLean Stevenson, and Alan Alda

In 2014, Radar's teddy bear fared well at $14,307.50 at One Of A Kind Collectibles Auctions. It was accompanied with a handwritten letter from Burghoff stating it was the one and only teddy bear used in the show.

Radar's teddy bear (*Photo courtesy of One Of A Kind Collectibles Auctions*)

FEBRUARY 29, 2004: *The Lord of the Rings: The Return of the King* won eleven Academy Awards, tying with *Ben-Hur* and *Titanic* for the most Oscars (filmsite.org).

In 2014, Aragorn's sword used by Viggo Mortensen in the movie excelled at $437,000 at Bonhams. One of four created, it was made for close-ups and not used in battle scenes. Director Peter Jackson presented the sword to Christopher Lee for his advice during production. Lee appeared as "Saruman" in all of *The Lord of the Rings* movies and in the last two *Hobbit* movies.

"Sting," the sword of Bilbo and Frodo Baggins used by Elijah Wood, sold for $161,000, and Sauron's helmet, worn by actor Sala Baker, earned $41,600 at Julien's Auctions in 2013.

Viggo Mortensen (*Photo courtesy of Nicolas Genin*)

MARCH

MARCH 1, 1941: Captain America exploded upon the comic book scene by punching Hitler in the jaw in his first officially published appearance in *Captain America Comics #1* (marvel. com). A CGC 9.2 rated copy hit $343,057 in 2011 at Comicconnect.com. A CGC VF+ 8.5 copy sold for $95,600 at Heritage Auctions in 2009. Created by Joe Simon and Jack Kirby, this issue sold extremely well then, and Captain America currently sells well at the box office. *Captain America: Civil War* (2016) has made more than $1 billion worldwide (the-numbers.com) to date.

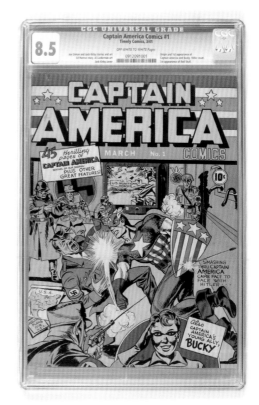

Captain America Comics #1 (Photo courtesy of Heritage Auctions, HA.com)

MARCH 2, 1793: Military leader and politician Sam Houston was born. He is the only person ever to be elected governor of two states: Tennessee and Texas. While not at the Alamo, Houston did defeat Gen. Santa Anna at San Jacinto, securing the independence of Texas from Mexico.

A Bowie knife Houston carried in the Battle of San Jacinto brought $297,000 in 2002 from an anonymous buyer (freerepublic.com, 12/28/2).

Sam Houston

MARCH 3, 1847: Born in Scotland, Alexander Graham Bell believed his greatest invention was—the photophone, a machine for transmitting voice messages via beam of light. He demonstrated a working photophone in 1880. An eight-page letter to his parents dated June 10, 1878 and describing how to ground their phone line that had suffered a lightning strike, also containing his drawings, gaveled at $94,430.40 in 2012 at RR Auction.

Alexander Graham Bell

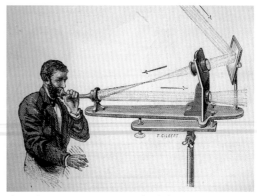

Photophone transmitting voice by light

MARCH 4, 1888: The birthday of "Win just one for the Gipper" Knute Rockne in Norway. No other college football coach has matched or beaten his thirteen-year record of 105-12-5 or winning percentage of .881 (sports-reference.com). Rockne died in a plane crash in March 31, 1931 on a commercial flight after a wing fell off the plane.

Knute Rockne

His handwritten plays (*Photo courtesy of Heritage Auctions, HA.com*)

The Gipper

In 2015, Knute Rockne's handwritten plays on his personal stationery, from the 1920s and including passing plays, scored $17,925 at Heritage auctions. Rockne was an innovator with the forward pass.

George "The Gipper" Gipp, one of Rockne's greatest and most versatile players at Notre Dame, died in 1920 at the age of twenty-five from a streptococcal infection.

MARCH 5, 1770: *The Boston Massacre*, a print of the engraving by Paul Revere, *The Bloody Massacre Perpetrated in King Street, Boston, on March 5th 1770, by Party of the 29th REGt.*, auctioned for $146,500 in 2012 at Christie's. It did not depict the event as it actually happened, but it did help instigate the Revolutionary War. Crispus Attucks and four others died in the conflict (bostonmassacre.net).

A copy of Paul Revere's engraving in the Library of Congress

MARCH 5, 1963: Patsy Cline died in a plane crash in inclement weather in Tennessee. Her manager Randy Hughes, who was not instrument-trained, was the pilot. He and two others also died. Cline's hits included: "Walkin' After Midnight," "Crazy," and "I Fall to Pieces."

At a 2002 Profiles in History auction, her dice-motif dress made $7,500.

Patsy Cline

MARCH 6, 1836: The Alamo fell. In 2014, British rock star Phil Collins donated to the Alamo his 200-piece collection of artifacts from that famous battle and from the 1835-1836 Texas War for Independence. Worth $10-

Davy Crockett's knife used at the Alamo, displayed in the San Jacinto Museum of History *(Photo courtesy of Brian Reading; it was not part of Collins' collection)*

(Continued on the next page.)

Davy Crockett (*Photo courtesy of cliff1066*)

Jim Bowie

Phil Collins

$15 million, it included a Davy Crockett rifle, Jim Bowie's knife, General Santa Anna's sword, and letters from William Travis, commander of the Alamo (dallasnews.com, 10/28/14).

MARCH 6, 1475: Michelangelo was born. While in his twenties, he sculpted the *David* and the *Pieta*, which depicts Mary holding the crucified Christ.

In 1972, Laszlo Toth attacked the *Pieta* with a hammer, breaking off Mary's left arm and part of her nose and chipping an eyelid. Ruled insane, Toth was not charged. The *Pieta* was restored.

Michelangelo

Pieta (*Photo courtesy of Juan Romero*)

Laszlo Toth (*bottom right*) being subdued by patrons

MARCH 7, 1876: Alexander Graham Bell was granted a patent for the telephone, and he changed the world. Many inventors also worked on the technology and

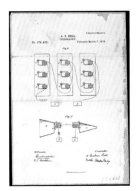

Bell's original patent illustration for his telephone

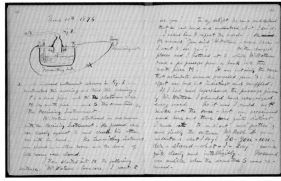

Bell's notebook in the Library of Congress describing his first successful experiment with the telephone

created sound-communicating devices. Some copied the designs of Bell and others to create their own phones, as did Lars Magnus Ericsson. A Skeleton Phone he made and marketed about 1884 went for about $12,700 (8,874.25 Euros) in 2011 by Auction Team Breker.

Ericsson's Skeleton Phone (*Photo © 2016 by AUCTION TEAM BREKER, Cologne, Germany, www.Breker.com*)

MARCH 8, 2000: Fifty-five, gold-plated Oscars being shipped to the Motion Picture Academy were stolen in Los Angeles by two workers of a trucking company. Local police and the FBI joined the desperate search to find them before Oscar Night, and on March 19, Willie Fulgear found fifty-two of them in ten packing crates left in and around a dumpster. He received a reward of $50,000, tickets to the ceremony, and was introduced on stage by host Billy Crystal (vanityfair.com, 4/4/01). The thieves were caught.

This isn't the only instance of missing Oscars. Of the 3,000+ awarded since 1929, seventy have been stolen and sixty-seven found—including Whoopi Goldberg's for Best Supporting Actress for *Ghost*. While in transit to have the gold plating restored, someone opened the package, took out the Oscar, and for some reason, sent the empty package on to the company. The possibility of jail time probably occurred to the thief who dumped the statue in an airport trash can where it was found (vanityfair.com, 2/19/16).

MARCH 9, 1934: Soviet Cosmonaut Yuri Gagarin was born, and twenty-seven years later, he was the first person to enter outer space. He died on March 27, 1968 in the crash of his MiG-15 during a training flight.

In 2014, a signed 1961 *LIFE* magazine cover featuring him and Nikita Khrushchev sold for $3,250 at Heritage Auctions.

Yuri (*l.*) on the cover of *LIFE* (*Photo courtesy of Heritage Auctions, HA.com*)

MARCH 10, 1913: Born c. 1822, Araminta Ross (Harriet Tubman) passed away this day after a lifetime of service to others as a conductor on the Underground Railroad, as a Union scout, spy, and nurse during the Civil War, and as an abolitionist and suffragette.

In 2010, her signed hymnal and a shawl given to her by Queen Victoria were donated to the Smithsonian (smithsonanmag.com, Sept. 2010).

Harriet Tubman

MARCH 11, 1958: The Air Force dropped a nuclear bomb on Mars Bluff, S.C.—accidentally. Fortunately, it had no nuclear materials, but unfortunately, it did contain explosives. Six people were injured in the explosion. The accident happened while the navigator/bombardier was checking for a faulty locking pin, and he grabbed the release pin by mistake.

In 2002, the autographed, eleven-page logbook of co-pilot Captain Robert A. Lewis of the B-29 *Enola Gay* auctioned for $391,000 at Christie's. Titled, "Bombing of Hiroshima Aug. 6, 1945," it recorded a minute-by-minute account of the dropping of the first atomic bomb on Hiroshima.

MARCH 12, 1894: Coca-Cola was sold in bottles for the first time. Until then, it was dispensed from a soda fountain into glasses. In 2011, a contour Coca-Cola prototype bottle, only one of two known to exist and designed by Earl R. Dean in 1915, sold for $250,000 at Julien's Live. It was not rolled out into production due to the bottle's fat middle making it unstable on conveyor belts, but a slimmed-down model's shape has become iconic.

One of the two Coca-Cola contour bottle prototypes
(*Photo courtesy of Gavinmacqueen*)

MARCH 13, 1881: Alexander III (Romanov) became Emperor of Russia after the assassination of his father. He and his son Nicholas II commissioned about fifty Imperial Eggs from Peter Faberge for their wives. In 2014, a previously missing Tsar Nicholas Egg changed hands privately for $33 million after being found

The found Imperial Egg contained a Vacheron Constantin clock that popped up as the surprise. (*Photos, courtesy of and copyright © Wartski, 2014; photography by Prudence Cuming Associates*)

by a scrap metal dealer and purchased for about $13,000 (cnn.com, 6/29/15).

MARCH 14, 1879: Albert Einstein was born. In 1926, he and engineer/physicist Leo Szilard invented, of all things, a refrigerator. It had no moving parts and cooled with only a heat source. A family dying due to gas escaping from an early model refrigerator prompted this invention.

Szilard later developed the concept of the chain reaction, and his writings led to the Manhattan Project. In 2015, twenty-seven letters written by Einstein yielded $420,625 at Profiles in History.

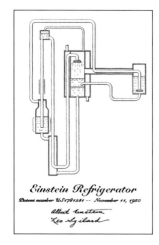

Einstein Refrigerator
Patent number US1781541 -- November 11, 1930
Albert Einstein
Leo Szilard

The patent application diagram for Einstein and Szilard's refrigerator

MARCH 15, 1999: Inducted into the Rock and Roll Hall of Fame this day were: Bruce Springsteen, Paul McCartney, Billy Joel, Curtis Mayfield, Del Shannon, Dusty Springfield, and The Staple Singers.

In 2014, Bruce Springsteen auctioned off a lasagna dinner at his home (you read that correctly, a lasagna dinner) to benefit Stand Up For Heroes. The dinner sold for $300,000. He also sold a one-hour guitar lesson, a ride in his motorcycle's sidecar, and two guitars for another $300,000 donated to the charity.

Bruce Springsteen (*Photo courtesy of Laura Bland*)

MARCH 16, 1926: The original Nutty Professor (the one before Eddie Murphy), Jerry Lewis, was born. Actor, comedian, and partner with Dean Martin in many movies, Lewis served as the National Chairman of the Muscular Dystrophy Association and hosted an annual March of Dimes Telethon, raising about $2.6 billion over six decades.

In 2016, a Norman Rockwell oil and

Cinderfella artwork (*Photo courtesy of Heritage Auctions, HA.com*)

pencil on canvas created for promotional art for the Jerry Lewis movie, *Cinderfella*, signed by Rockwell, sold for $250,000 at Heritage Auctions.

MARCH 17, 1902: Birthday cake for golfing legend Bobby Jones. In 1930, he won all four major championships and achieved a Grand Slam. This was prior to the creation of the Masters, but even so, no other player but he has won a Grand Slam in one calendar year.

Bobby Jones

His Green Jacket (Photo courtesy of Heritage Auctions, HA.com)

Bobby Jones' 1937 Augusta Green Jacket scored $310,700 at Heritage Auctions in 2011. Rarely are Green Jackets sold because Augusta National does not allow them to leave the grounds—except for a year, then the winner must return it (augusta.com, 4/12/15).

MARCH 18, 1937: Jim the Wonder Dog passed away in Marshall, Missouri. A black and white English setter, Jim was able to predict: the winner of the Kentucky Derby seven years in a row; the winner of the 1936 World Series (the Yankees); Roosevelt winning the presidency in 1936 over Landon; and the sex of babies to be born. He found cars by their license plate numbers and people by their color of clothing. He understood directions—both spoken and written—in Spanish, French, Greek, German, and English. (His owner Sam Van Arsdale only spoke English.) Jim was examined by veterinary professionals, but no one, including Van Arsdale, could figure out how he did the impossible (ruralmissouri.org).

1936 Kentucky Derby program signed by Babe Ruth (Photo courtesy of Heritage Auctions, HA. com)

(Continued on the next page.)

A park with a bronze statue of Jim is dedicated to him in Marshall. Although he received many lucrative offers, Van Arsdale never used Jim for profit.

In 2015, a 1936 Kentucky Derby program signed by Babe Ruth sold for $1,912 at Heritage Auctions.

MARCH 18, 1990: Rembrandt's *The Storm on the Sea of Galilee* and a self-portrait were stolen from the Isabella Gardner Museum along with Vermeer's *The Concert* and a finial from the top of a Napoleonic flag staff (gardnermuseum.org). Two men dressed as Boston policemen took a total of thirteen pieces of art, including work by Manet and Degas. *The Concert* is valued at $200+ million; none of the works of art have been recovered to date.

The Storm on the Sea of Galilee

MARCH 19, 1953: Francis Crick wrote a letter to his son Michael about his discovery of DNA's structure. That letter sold for $6,098,500 at Christie's.

MARCH 20, 1952: At the 24th Academy Awards, *A Streetcar Named Desire* won Oscars for Vivien Leigh (Best Actress), Karl Malden (Best Supporting Actor), and Kim Hunter (Best Supporting Actress). *An American in Paris* won Best Motion Picture, and Humphrey Bogart won Best Actor for *The African Queen*. The real *African Queen*, a 100+-year-old, steam-powered boat, was rescued from a scrapheap in 2012 by a couple who refurbished it and use it for sailing tours (cnn.com, 5/2/12).

Karl Malden

In 2006, a fake Karl Malden Best Supporting Actor Oscar was posted for sale on eBay for $30,000. All Oscars have a serial number, and this one had the correct one, SN: 626. The seller said he found it in a dumpster, broken at the ankles, when he was a kid. No records of a duplicate of

Malden's Oscar exist (goldderby.latimes.com, 10/5/05). The statue was removed from the website before the close of the sale.

MARCH 20, 1973: The Baseball Writers' Association of America held a special election to waive the five-year waiting period to vote on Roberto Clemente for the Baseball Hall of Fame. Clemente had arranged relief flights to Managua, Nicaragua, after an earthquake, but

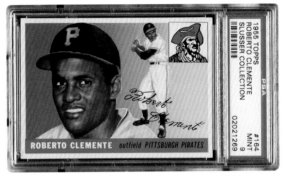

Roberto Clemente's rookie card (*Photo courtesy of Heritage Auctions, HA.com*)

corrupt officials diverted the aid. He boarded the fourth relief flight on December 31, 1973 to ensure its delivery, but the overloaded plane went down in the Atlantic. He was thirty-eight.

In eighteen seasons with the Pittsburgh Pirates, Roberto Clemente had 3,000 hits, 240 home runs, 1,305 RBIs and a batting average of .317. Clemente was an All-Star fifteen times, World Series champion twice, Series MVP once, and a National League MVP. He also earned twelve Gold Glove Awards and was NL batting champion four times. He was inducted into the Hall of Fame in 1973.

In 2016, a 1955 Topps Roberto Clemente #164 rookie baseball card PSA-rated Mint 9 topped out at $488,000 at Heritage Auctions.

MARCH 21, 1939: America's most popular singer at one time, Kate Smith recorded Irving Berlin's "God Bless America" for RCA Victor on this day. Celine Deon and LeAnn Rimes have also recorded this patriotic song. Played at many sporting events, the Philadelphia Flyers deemed it good luck for their hockey team in the 1970s (parademagazine.com, 8/6/13) when they won their only Stanley Cups in the 1973–1974 and 1974–1975 seasons.

A thirteen-inch, 1974–75 Philadelphia Flyers Mini Stanley Cup Championship trophy belonging to goalie Bernie Parent and inscribed with team members' names sold for $8,365 at Heritage Auctions in 2015.

1974-75 Mini Stanley Cup (*Photo courtesy of Heritage Auctions, HA.com*)

MARCH 22, 1894: The first Stanley Cup Championship was played in Canada. The Montreal Amateur Athletic Association beat the Ottawa Capitals, 3-1.

MARCH 22, 1599: Flemish master artist Sir Anthony Van Dyck was born. Although known throughout the world for the famous facial hair bearing his name that has been sported by the likes of Custer, Lenin, Buffalo Bill, Colonel Sanders, Johnny Depp, Christian Bale, and even Pierce Brosnan at one time, Van Dyck was court painter for King Charles I of England and a master portrait painter. Even so, his 1640 *Self Portrait* holds the record for all of his work; it yielded $13,521,704 at Sotheby's in 2009.

A Van Dyck selfie, but not the record-holder

MARCH 23, 1775: Patrick Henry gave his famous speech saying, "Give me liberty or give me death," which also helped to inspire the American Revolution.

A Patrick Henry autographed letter sold for $2,390 in 2008 at Heritage Auctions.

Patrick Henry

MARCH 23-24, 2012: Heritage Auctions sold the Berwick Discovery Of Lost Movie Posters for $503,000+. The thirty-three Berwick posters were found in an attic and later bought at a small auction in Berwick, Penn. A few in this treasure trove were: a 1931 *Dracula* Style F one sheet at $143,400; a *Cimarron* one sheet, $101,575; a *Stagecoach* one sheet, $56,763; a *Casablanca* one sheet, $28,680; and a *Tarzan and His Mate* lobby streamer, $26,290.

Tarzan and His Mate lobby streamer (*Photo courtesy of Heritage Auctions, HA.com*)

MARCH 24, 1930: Steve McQueen came into the world with a talent for acting and a need for speed. Starring in some must-see movies like *The Great Escape, Papillon*, and *The Magnificent Seven*, McQueen also amassed a great car and motorcycle collection. The star of it, perhaps, was his 1915 Cyclone Board Track Racer motorcycle, capable of 100+ mph. It roared off for $852,500 at Mecum Auctions in 2014 (gizmag. com, 10/14/14)

Steve McQueen

Steve McQueen's Cyclone; note the pedal and chain (*Photo courtesy of Mecum Auctions*)

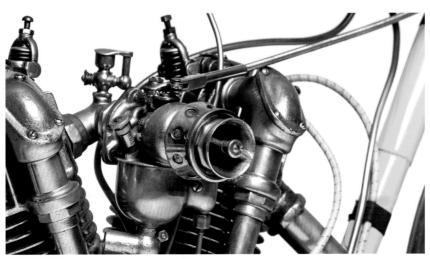

The Cyclone's engine (*Photo courtesy of Mecum Auctions*)

MARCH 25, 1905: The War Department returned Confederate battle flags captured during the Civil War to states and hometowns. It required an act of Congress under President Theodore Roosevelt for this to happen.

Confederate battle flags are highly collectible. The highest paid to date was for General J.E.B. Stuart's battle flag sewn by his wife that sold for $956,000 at Heritage Auctions in 2006. A Confederate "Liberty or Death" flag captured by George Armstrong Custer's Cavalry from Stuart's Cavalry during their retreat from Gettysburg in 1863 auctioned for $107,550 in 2007 at Heritage Auctions.

J.E.B. Stuart's battle flag (*Photo courtesy of Heritage Auctions, HA. com*)

The captured Stuart Cavalry flag (*Photo courtesy of Heritage Auctions, HA.com*)

MARCH 26, 1937: A six-foot-tall concrete statue of Popeye was erected in Crystal City, Texas, during the 2nd Annual Spinach Festival. In 2014, Jeff Koons' *Popeye* hit $28,165,000 at Sotheby's. The sculpture is mirror-polished, stainless steel with transparent color coating and measures 78 x 51.75 x 18.5 inches. Signed and dated 2009–2011, it is the third in an edition of three plus an artist's proof.

MARCH 26: Ludwig van Beethoven passed away in 1827. Born this day were poet Robert Frost in 1874 (winner of four Pulitzer Prizes) and Thomas Lanier "Tennessee" Williams in 1911 (*Cat on a Hot Tin Roof, A Streetcar Named Desire*).

B. Traven (not his real name) died in 1969. Traven was actually Ret Marut, a German actor, writer, and anarchist who fled Europe to Mexico in 1924; he was the author of the novel *The Treasure of Sierra Madre*. The movie adaptation with

Humphrey Bogart won three Academy Awards: two for John Huston for Directing and for Adapted Screenplay, and one for his father Walter Huston for Best Supporting Actor—the first father-son win (IMDb.com).

An Italian movie poster of the film made $5,497 in 2016 at Heritage Auctions.

Robert Frost, c. 1910

Tennessee Williams

B. Traven/Ret Marut

Ludwig van Beethoven

Italian movie poster for *The Treasure of Sierra Madre* (*Photo courtesy of Heritage Auctions, HA.com*)

MARCH 27, 1850: A twenty-two-pound gold nugget was found by Dr. Thadeus Hildreth and prospectors with him in California.

The largest recorded gold nugget discovered to date was the Welcome Stranger nugget weighing 173 lbs. It was found in Victoria, Australia, in 1869 and melted down into ingots.

Large intact nuggets bring premium prices, such as the Butte Nugget found in California that weighed 6.07 lbs. It sold to a private buyer in 2014 for an undisclosed amount—but the asking price was $400,000 (sfgate.com, 10/25/14).

A woodcut of The Welcome Stranger Nugget

MARCH 28, 1990: Olympic gold medalist Jesse Owens was posthumously awarded the Congressional Gold Medal by President George H.W. Bush. Owens passed away March 31, 1980. In 1976, President Gerald Ford awarded him the Presidential Medal of Freedom.

Jesse Owens' Olympic medal, front and back (*Photos courtesy of SCP Auctions*)

At the 1936 Berlin Olympics in front of Adolf Hitler and Nazis, he won gold medals in four events: one hundred meters, 200 meters, 4×100-meter relay and long jump.

In 2013, one of Owens' Olympic gold medals (it is not known for which event) sold for $1,466,574 at SCP Auctions.

Jesse Owens at the 1936 Olympics

MARCH 29, 1867: When Cy Young was born on this day, the Great Umpire in the Sky yelled, "Play ball!" One of the greatest Major League pitchers ever, he still holds the record for most wins with 511; Walter Johnson trails quite a way back at 417.

Denton True Young earned his nickname

Cy Young

Cy Young's 1908 Red Sox jersey shirt (*Photo courtesy of Heritage Auctions, HA.com*)

"Cy" from using his fastball against fences and making them look like they'd been hit by a cyclone. He started with the Cleveland Spiders in 1890, and over his twenty-two seasons, he threw 2,803 strikeouts, pitched 7,356 innings, and had a 2.63 earned run average. He was a World Series champion in 1903. The year after his death in 1955, the Cy Young Award was instituted and awarded annually to the best ML pitcher. In 1967, it was awarded to the best pitcher in both leagues.

In 2011, Cy Young's 1908 game-worn Boston Red Sox uniform scored at $657,250 at Heritage Auctions.

MARCH 30, 1853: Birthday of Vincent Van Gogh. Recognized now as a great artist—but never during his lifetime—Van Gogh was a voracious reader, and he also translated sections of the Bible into French, German, and English (www. vggallery.com). His *Portrait*

Portrait of Dr. Gachet

Van Gogh's self-portrait

of Dr. Gachet sold for $82.5 million in 1990 at Christie's (articles.latime.com, 5/16/90).

MARCH 31, 1685: Birthday cake for Johann Sebastian Bach, father of twenty children. In 2014, Christie's auctioned a section of an autograph manuscript of church cantata BWV 188, "Ich habe meine Zuversicht," c. October 1728, for $347,746.

Bach

MARCH 31, 1878: Jack Johnson, the first African American to earn the title of heavy-weight boxing champion, was born in Galveston, Texas. A special award to him from an Australian jeweler and inscribed, "World's Heavyweight Champion, Black Opal Trophy, Presented by Percy Marks, Won by Jack Johnson, Sydney, Dec. 26, 1908," made $28,680 at Heritage Auctions in 2011.

Jack Johnson

The Black Opal Trophy (*Photo courtesy of Heritage Auctions, HA.com*)

APRIL

APRIL 1, 2009: The Post Office announced Bart, Homer, Lisa, Maggie, and Marge Simpson would each be featured on a new stamp and that one billion *Simpsons* stamps would be printed. In an April Fools' joke on the American taxpayer, only 318 million eventually sold, resulting in $1.2 million lost in printing costs (bloomberg.com, 8/21/12). In 2015, Heritage Auctions sold one of The Simpsons Limited Edition cels created for

(Photo courtesy of Heritage Auctions, HA.com)

their one hundredth episode, featuring thirty-two of the characters trying to fit on the couch, for $1,434. Ten artist proofs and one hundred cels were made of this image.

APRIL 2, 1805: Fairy tale spinner, as well as poetry, novel, and travelogue writer, Hans Christian Andersen was born in Denmark. Anderson's other great talent was cutting paper into intricate designs, which he then used to tell stories. One of his signed and inscribed papercuts

H.C. Andersen

An H.C. Andersen papercut *(Photo courtesy of www.museum.odense.dk)*

from 1874 with ballet dancers, windmill men, flowers, heart-shaped windows, sandmen, storks, and gnomes hammered for $21,250 in 2009 at Christie's.

APRIL 3, 1882: While his back was turned, the outlaw Jesse James was shot and killed by Bob Ford, a member of his own gang, to get a $10,000 reward. A Jesse James wanted poster took $57,475 in 2012 at Lebel's Old West Auction.

Bob Ford

Jesse James

APRIL 3, 1860: Pony Express riders hit the trail for the first time for a ten-day ride from Missouri to California. The cost to deliver a half-ounce letter was $5 (about $133 today). The price decreased substantially later. Even so, the telegraph put the Pony Express out of business after only eighteen months. An envelope dated "July 22d" (1860) bearing a 10¢ pale green stamp sold for $200,000 at Robert Siegel Auctions in 2013. It was originally stolen in transit and recovered two years later. Pony Express envelopes, or covers, often sell for tens of thousands of dollars. This one had rare history in its price.

The Pony Express cover (*Photo courtesy of Robert Siegel Auctions*)

APRIL 4, 2012: A 900-year-old Chinese ceramic Song Dynasty Ruyao washer bowl auctioned for $26,770,289 at Sotheby's in Hong Kong. It was made for a Chinese emperor for washing calligraphy brushes.

Ru Guanyao lobed brush washer (*Photos courtesy of Sotheby's*)

APRIL 5, 1856: Booker T. Washington was born. He said, "Associate yourself with people of good quality, for it is better to be alone than in bad company" (brainyquote.com). A typed letter to MIT President Henry Pritchett in 1900 on the letterhead of Tuskegee Normal and Industrial Institute and signed by Booker T. Washington went for $350 on vintagememorabilia.com, c. 2008.

Booker T. Washington

APRIL 6, 1520: The great Renaissance artist and architect Raphael, or Raffaello Sanzio, passed away at the age of thirty-seven. A prolific artist, three of his master-pieces include *The School of Athens, Sistine Madonna,* and *Saint George and the Dragon.* In 2012, his black chalk sketch, *Head of a Young Apostle,* gaveled for $47,869,045 at Sotheby's.

Sistine Madonna

Raphael's selfie

Head of a Young Apostle
(Photo courtesy of Sotheby's)

APRIL 7, 2016: Seven paintings from Andy Warhol's Campbell Soup Series were stolen from the Springfield Art Museum in Springfield, Missouri (nbcnews.com, 4/12/16). In 2015, three prints from his Endangered Species Series and six from Ten Portraits of Jews of the Twentieth Century were discovered stolen from a California movie company—they had been replaced with color copies years before. Two were returned to police and one was sold through an auction house (telegraph. co.uk, 9/16/15).

(Continued on the next page.)

In 2009, ten screen prints from Warhol's *Athlete Series* were stolen from the home of a Warhol friend who commissioned eight sets of the paintings (seattletimes. com, 10/13/09), which featured: Muhammad Ali, O.J. Simpson, Dorothy Hamill, Pelé, Jack Nicklaus, Kareem Abdul-Jabbar, Tom Seaver, Willie Shoemaker, Chris Evert, and Rod Gilbert. One set sold at Christie's in 2011 for $5,682,500. In 2007, *Muhammad Ali* from the series auctioned for $9,225,000 at Christie's. Andy Warhol passed away on Feb. 22, 1987.

APRIL 8, 1974: With his 715th home run this day, Hank Aaron beat Babe Ruth's home run record. Aaron hit 755 homers in his career. In 1999, his 755th home run ball sold for $650,000 at Guernsey's (usatoday30.usatoday.com, 7/25/07).

Hank Aaron holding his 755th home run ball (*Photo courtesy of Guernsey's*)

APRIL 9, 1865: General Robert E. Lee surrendered to General Ulysses S. Grant at Appomattox Courthouse, officially ending the Civil War. Present at those proceedings was twenty-five-year-old Brevet Major General George Armstrong Custer.

Custer's personal cavalry swallowtail battle flag, sewn by his wife Elizabeth Custer, brought $896,250 at Heritage Auctions in 2007. Custer received the flag

Custer's battle flag (*Photo courtesy of Heritage Auctions, HA.com*)

during a battle at Dinwiddie Court House near Petersburg, Virginia, on March 31, 1865.

Cadet Custer at West Point, c. 1859

George and Elizabeth

APRIL 9, 1959: America's first astronauts were announced by NASA. The careers of this elite group spanned the Mercury, Gemini, Apollo, and Space Shuttle programs.

A 10 x 8-inch black-and-white photograph of the Mercury 7 (as they are called) taken on July 12, 1962 sold for $11,950 in 2007 at Heritage Auctions. It was autographed by all: (back row) Alan B. Shepard, Jr., Walter M. Schirra, Jr., John H. Glenn, Jr., and (front) Virgil I. Grissom, M. Scott Carpenter, Donald K. Slayton, and Leroy G. Cooper, Jr.

The autographed photo of the Mercury 7 (*Photo courtesy of Heritage Auctions, HA.com*)

APRIL 10, 1896: The first modern Olympic Summer Games marathon was run from Marathon to Athens, Greece, and won by Greek Spyridon Louis. He was awarded the Brèal Silver Cup, which was designed by French author Michel Brèal who also recommended the marathon be run in the footsteps of the Greek messenger Pheidippides.

A Brèal Silver Cup went for $860,000 at Christie's in 2012. Spyridon competed in no other running events afterwards.

Spyridon Louis

APRIL 11, 1970: Apollo 13 launched. An oxygen tank explosion curtailed the mission to the moon and threatened to take the lives of the crew, but James Lovell, Jack Swigert, and Fred Haise returned safely to Earth on the 17th.

Lovell's notebook with his calculations that helped to save their lives landed a top bid of $388,375 at Heritage Auctions in 2011 (csmonitor.com, 12/1/11). However, NASA halted the auction, questioning Lovell's ownership of it. This had happened before to auctions of space memorabilia, so Congress passed a law allowing astronauts to keep their gear (space.com, 9/27/12).

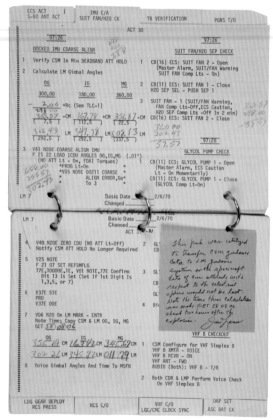

Lovell's checklist (*Photo courtesy of Heritage Auctions, HA.com*)

APRIL 11, 2016: Han Solo's leather jacket from *Star Wars: The Force Awakens* blasted off for $191,000 at an ifonly.com auction to benefit FACES (Finding a Cure for Epilepsy and Seizures). Harrison Ford's daughter suffers from epilepsy (time.com, 4/13/16).

APRIL 12, 1861: The Civil War began. By the end, a calculated 618,222 soldiers lost their lives: 360,222 from the Union and 258,000 from the Confederacy. But in 2012, new research using 19th century census data increased the amount of total dead to between 650,000 and 850,000, probably about 750,000 (nyt.com, 4/2/12). It is believed that for every three men who died in battle, another five died of disease (civilwar.org).

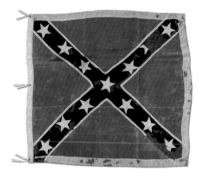

9th Virginia Cavalry flag (*Photo courtesy of James D. Julia Auctioneers, Fairfield, ME, www.jamesdjulia.com*)

In 2013, James Julia Auctions sold the battle flag of the 9th Virginia Cavalry for $82,225.

APRIL 13, 1743: Thomas Jefferson was born. Not surprising that letters signed by the lead writer of the Declaration of Independence are in demand. An 1812 letter signed by him sold for $218,500 in 2011 at Christie's.

Thomas Jefferson, 1786

APRIL 14, 1912: The *Titanic* struck the iceberg. The ship sank early the next morning, and more than 1,500 people lost their lives of the 2,224 passengers and crew on board.

A two-handled, sterling silver loving cup that survivor Molly Brown awarded

(Continued on the next page.)

Captain Arthur Rostron receiving the cup from Molly Brown, 1912

to the Arthur Rostron, captain of the rescue ship *Carpathia*, sold for $197,982 at Henry Aldridge & Son in 2015 (paulfrasercollectibles.com). A captain for the Cunard Line, Rostron also received a Congressional Gold Medal.

Left & Right: *Titanic* menu *(Photos courtesy of Heritage Auctions, HA.com)*

The iceberg

The only known first class dinner menu from the last meal on the *Titanic* secured $118,750 at Heritage Auctions in November 2015. Five men at the same table signed it and added their addresses; four of them eventually survived.

A photo of the iceberg auctioned for more than $32,000 in 2015 at Henry Aldridge & Son (nypost.com, 10/24/15).

APRIL 15, 1452: Leonardo da Vinci's birthday. A true Renaissance man and acknowledged scientific genius, inventor (parachute, helicopter, tank), and master of the arts (*Mona Lisa, The Last Supper*), his *Salvator Mundi*—which had been attributed to an artist in his studio and previously auctioned for about $10,000—sold for between $75 million and $80 million in a private sale in 2014 (nytimes.com, 3/9/2014).

Salvator Mundi

APRIL 15, 1865: President Abraham Lincoln died after being shot by assassin John Wilkes Booth the day before. The Deringer* owned and used by Booth is on display at Ford's Theater in Washington, D.C., along with: the boot Dr. Samuel Mudd cut from

Booth's Deringer (*Photo courtesy of Library of Congress*)

Booth's broken ankle; Booth's 1864 pocket diary; his compass; life masks made of Abraham Lincoln in 1860 and 1865; and many more artifacts. In his pocket diary, Booth wrote: "Our country owed all her troubles to him, and God simply made me the instrument of his punishment" (fords.org).

In 1825, Henry Deringer created a small pistol, and those made by his company are spelled with a capital "D" and only one "r". Later, any small pistol was called a "derringer" and spelled this way.

APRIL 16, 1889: Silent film star Charlie Chaplin was born, and on April 6, 1916, he really celebrated—after signing a contract with Mutual Film Corporation for a salary of $670,000 ($15+ million today) to make twelve movies. He was knighted in 1975 by Queen Elizabeth II and became Sir Charles Spencer Chaplin.

In 2011, Profiles in History sold one of his bowler hats worn in films for $135,300.

The Little Tramp resorting to eating his boot in *The Gold Rush*, 1925

The real Charlie Chaplin

APRIL 17, 1790: Benjamin Franklin passed away.

In 2009, a copy of his *Poor Richard's Almanac*, officially titled then, "Poor Richard, 1733. An Almanack for the Year of Christ 1733," along with two other almanac volumes, auctioned for $566,500 at Sotheby's. It is one of three known to exist, and while in publication from 1732 to 1758, his almanac sold well. It contained puzzles, weather forecasts, household tips, and Franklin's witty sayings like: "He's a Fool that makes his Doctor his Heir."

A 1739 copy of *Poor Richard's Almanack*

APRIL 18, 1998: Michael Jordan played his final regular season game. The Chicago Bulls jersey he wore then sold for $173,240 at Goldin Auctions in 2015.

APRIL 18, 2015: The gray dress worn by Scarlett O'Hara in the Shanty Town scene in *Gone With The Wind* went for $137,000 at Heritage Auctions. It was found on the floor of a costume company, about to be thrown out, and purchased by James Tumblin for $20. He had worked for Universal Studios, and he saw the label in it imprinted with "Selznick International Pictures" and "Scarlett production dress" (cnn.com, 4/22/15).

The $20 dress (*Photo courtesy of Heritage Auctions, HA.com*)

APRIL 19, 1775: The Battles of Lexington and Concord, the first battles of the Revolutionary War. A powder horn carried by Minuteman Oliver Buttrick in the Battle of Concord inscribed, "Oliver Buttrick, OCT. 1774," sold for $88,875 in 2016 at James Julia Auctions. Ralph Waldo Emerson wrote of this first battle as the "shot heard round the world" in his poem, "Concord Hymn."

Oliver Buttrick's powder horn carried in the Battle of Concord
(*Photo courtesy of James D. Julia Auctioneers, Fairfield, ME,*
www.jamesdjulia.com)

Oliver Buttrick

APRIL 20, 1889: Adolf Hitler was born. He died by gunshot from his own hand ten days after his birthday on April 30, 1945.

He was also an artist—but not a very good one. Yet, a collection of fourteen of his paintings and drawings surprised at $450,000 at Weilder Auction House in Nuremberg, Germany, in 2015 (news.artnet.com, 6/22/15).

Star & Stripes
newspaper, May
2, 1945

APRIL 21, 1910: Samuel Clemens (Mark Twain) passed away. One of America's greatest humorists and authors (*The Adventures of Tom Sawyer* and *Adventures of Huckleberry Finn*), he said: "All you need in this life is ignorance and confidence,

(Continued on the next page.)

and then success is sure," and "A man who carries a cat by the tail learns something he can learn in no other way" (brainyquote. com).

Susy Clemens

Samuel Clemens at age 15

His unpublished, *A Family Sketch* (written for his oldest daughter, Susy, who died at the age of twenty-four of spinal meningitis), sold for $242,500 in 2010 at Sotheby's.

APRIL 22, 2005: Johnny Carson's Shure SM33 microphone from *The Tonight Show Starring Johnny Carson* went for $50,787.50 at Heritage Auctions. Known as "the king of late night television," Carson's show was the last one watched by millions of Americans before turning in; it ran from 1962 to 1992. His show won six

Johnny Carson

Johnny Carson's microphone
(*Photo courtesy of Heritage Auctions, HA.com*)

Primetime Emmy Awards, and he received the Presidential Medal of Freedom. An accomplished comedian, he said: "If life were fair, Elvis would be alive, and all the impersonators would be dead" (brainyquote.com).

APRIL 23, 1928: Child star and adult humanitarian Shirley Temple was born in Santa Monica, California. Known in the movies for her perpetually bubbly and buoyant personality, Shirley Temple helped keep hope alive during the Depression. She was the No. 1 star in America and the most popular person from 1935 to 1939—and this in the days of Clark Gable, Greta Garbo, and FDR (nytimes.com,

Shirley Temple in *Bright Eyes* (1931)

Her dress from *Stand Up and Cheer* (Photo courtesy of Theriault's)

2/11/14). After movies, she served as ambassador to Ghana and Czechoslovakia, and she represented the International Federation of Multiple Sclerosis Societies.

A 9.5-carat, deep blue diamond graded VVS2 (nearly perfect) belonging to Shirley Temple did not reach its reserve price of $25 million and did not sell at Sotheby's in 2016 (fortune.com, 4/20/16). It was purchased by her father for $7,210 to commemorate the 1940 debut of her movie, *The Blue Bird*, which was not as popular as *Heidi, Curly Top, The Little Princess,* and *Rebecca of Sunnybrook Farm* (IMDb.com).

In 2015, almost 600 costumes, dolls, and memorabilia of Shirley Temple's were auctioned by Theriault's. The red-and-white polka dot dress she wore in *Stand Up and Cheer* sold for $75,000 to her hometown Santa Monica History Museum.

APRIL 24, 1731: As a child, Daniel Defoe survived the Great Plague of London in 1665 that killed 70,000 and the Great Fire of London. He grew up to become an accomplished author before dying on this day.

Three first editions, volumes 1-3 published 1719-1720, of *The Life and Strange Surprizing Adventures of Robinson Crusoe, of York, Mariner* cruised to $18,365 in 2013 at Bonhams.

Daniel Defoe

APRIL 24, 1904: Birthday of artist Willem de Kooning. In 2015, his abstract painting, *Interchange*, skyrocketed to $300 million; it is listed as the highest price paid for a painting at this time.

Willem de Kooning

APRIL 25, 1917: The First Lady of Song Ella Fitzgerald debuted in the world, and during her career, she produced 200 albums and 2,000 songs. She won thirteen Grammy Awards and an additional Grammy for Lifetime Achievement (ellafitzgerald.com). She also was awarded the Kennedy Center for the Performing Arts Medal of Honor Award and the Presidential Medal of Freedom.

A concert poster with a 1970 sketch of Ella Fitzgerald by Picasso, inscribed and signed by her, auctioned for $19,608 at RR Auctions in 2013.

Ella Fitzgerald, 1945

APRIL 26, 1564: William Shakespeare's baptismal date; his exact birthdate is not definitely known but is believed to be April 23.

Only six of his signatures exist, and each is valued between $3 million (fantasticfives.com) and $5 million (most-expensive.com). Truly, no one really knows exactly what astronomical price Shakespeare's signature

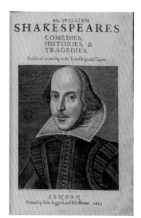

A First Folio

Shakespeare's six known signatures

would bring. However, a definite price was paid for one of the forty known and complete First Folios containing his plays—$5,153,242 in 2006 at Sotheby's.

APRIL 27, 1813: Ex⸝ ᵤᵣₑr and brigadier general during the War of 1812, Zebulon Pike was killed in the Battle of York (Ontario, Canada) on this day. Famous for the peak in Colorado bearing his name, he wrote of his expedition there, and the book was so popular it was translated into French, Dutch, and German. Cowan's Auctions sold a copy of it, *Zebulon Pike's Expeditions to the Sources of the Mississippi, 1805–1807*, for $7,800 in 2014.

APRIL 28, 1789: Lieutenant Fletcher Christian led a mutiny against Captain William Bligh on the *HMS Bounty*. Bligh and some of his loyal sailors eventually made it to England. Ten of the mutineers were later apprehended, brought back, and tried; three were hanged and seven were acquitted or pardoned. Fletcher Christian was never found but believed killed by Polynesians or by his own men.

In 2011, two of Captain Bligh's medals were auctioned for $216,000 at Noble Numismatics in Australia. One was a Naval Gold Medal for a victory against the Dutch and the other, also gold, was an award from the Society for the Encouragement of Arts, Manufactures and Commerce (the Royal Society of Arts) for returning to Tahiti and obtaining breadfruit, his original mission.

Bligh's medals, front and back
(Photos courtesy of Noble Numismatics)

Fletcher Christian and the mutineers seize HMS *Bounty*, engraving by Hablot Knight Browne, 1841

APRIL 29, 1954: Birthday cake for comedian and TV star Jerry Seinfeld.

In 2016, he did a little cleaning out of his garage and sold seventeen cars in his collection through Gooding & Co. for $22,244,500 (newsday.com, 3/21/16). Many were high-end Porsches, and the highlight was a 1955 Porsche Spyder that hit the road for $5,335,000. A couple of quirky cars: Seinfeld's 1964 Volkswagen Conversion Camper with less than 19,000 miles on it left for $99,000, and his 1960 Volkswagen Beetle went for $121,000.

APRIL 30, 1938: The first appearance of Happy Rabbit in *Porky's Hare Hunt*— the character that evolved into Bugs Bunny. Happy Rabbit was created initially by Ben Hardaway and Cal Dalton.

In 2015, a production cel from *What's Opera, Doc?* (1957) featuring Bugs and Elmer Fudd sold for $28,680 at Heritage Auctions.

What's Opera, Doc?
(Photo courtesy of Heritage
Auctions, HA.com)

MAY

MAY 1, 1967: Elvis Presley married Priscilla Ann Beaulieu at the Aladdin Hotel in Las Vegas.

In 2016, Graceland Auctions put up 100+ Elvis items for sale, and a pair of Elvis-worn prescription Nautic-style sunglasses by Neostyle sold for $8,750, and a 1969 signed and autographed photo of Elvis and Priscilla in Hawaii sold for $4,750. In 2014, Elvis' peacock jumpsuit sold for $245,000 at Sotheby's. It originally cost $10,000 to make it.

Elvis' and Priscilla's wedding photo

MAY 2, 1519: The great Leonardo da Vinci passed away. Reportedly, he requested sixty beggars to follow his casket during his funeral.

His manuscript or book of scientific writings known as the *Codex Leicester* is the most valuable manuscript in the world; it surpassed $30 million at Christie's in 1994 (close to $50 million today) and was sold to Bill Gates.

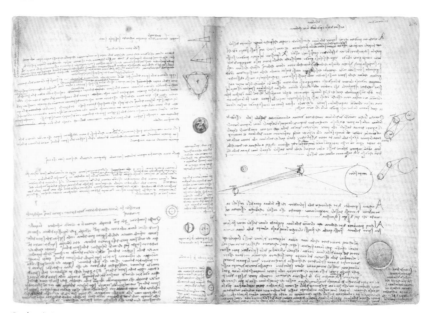

Codex Leicester

MAY 2, 2012: One of Edvard Munch's four versions of *The Scream*, a pastel on board in its original frame and dated 1895, was sold by Sotheby's for $119,922,500.

The Scream

MAY 3, 1937: Margaret Mitchell won the Pulitzer Prize for *Gone With The Wind* (pulitzer.org). AFI'S 100 Greatest Movie Quotes of All Time lists #1 as, "Frankly, my dear, I don't give a damn." (AFI.com) And, frankly, the word *frankly* was not in the book; it was added in the film.

Margaret Mitchell

MAY 4, 1929: Audrey Hepburn was born in Belgium of British parents.

The iconic "little black dress" she wore in *Breakfast at Tiffany's* auctioned at Christie's in 2006 for $923,187.

During WWII, Hepburn lived in the Netherlands and acted as a courier for the resistance for a time. She once said, "We saw young men put against the wall and shot, and they'd close the street and then open it, and you could pass by again. . . Don't discount anything awful you hear or read about the Nazis. It's worse than you could ever imagine." (*Audrey Hepburn* by Barry Paris, Penguin, 2001)

Audrey Hepburn

MAY 5, 1961: Alan Shepard Jr., blasted into space, the first American astronaut to do so. He was later scheduled to fly on the ill-fated Apollo 13 mission but was reassigned to Apollo 14. Shepard died on July 21, 1998 at the age of seventy-four from leukemia.

In 2011, RR Auction sold a three-page letter for $106,228 that he wrote to his parents a few months before he was chosen as a Mercury astronaut.

Alan Shepard in flight

MAY 6, 1931: Birth of the great Willie Mays. He slugged 660 home runs in his career. His 1951 Minneapolis Millers home jersey worn as he transitioned from the Negro Leagues to the Giants hit $44,063 at Robert Edward Auctions in 2011. On May 12, 2016, a 1952 Topps Willie Mays #261 rookie card graded PSA Mint 9 went over the fence for $478,000 at Heritage Auctions.

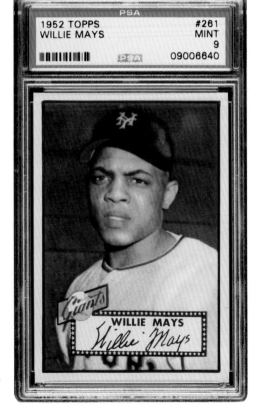

Willie Mays' 1952 rookie card (*Photo courtesy of Heritage Auctions, HA.com*)

MAY 6, 1937: LZ 129 *Hindenburg* caught fire while landing in Lakehurst, NJ; thirty-six people lost their lives.

A scorched envelope with four German 75pf stamps that were canceled on board sold for $15,000 at Robert Siegel Auctions in 2007.

The *Hindenburg*

MAY 7: The *Lusitania* was torpedoed by a German U-boat this day in 1915, and in WWII Germany surrendered to the Allies in 1945. Birthdays include: Gary Cooper, 1901; Johannes Brahms, 1833; Pyotr (Peter) Ilyich Tchaikovsky, 1840; and NFL quarterback and Super Bowl V champion Johnny Unitas, 1933.

Unitas' 1960s game jersey hammered for $103,500 at Hunt Auctions in 2015. A 1942 photo of Babe Ruth and Cooper from *The Pride of the Yankees* inscribed by the Babe to Cooper sold for $11,850 at Robert Edward Auctions in 2013.

Johnny Unitas

This 1942 promotional photo from *The Pride of the Yankees* of Cooper, Christy Walsh (the Babe's agent), and Ruth sold for $105.57 in 2010 at Heritage Auctions. (*Photo courtesy of Heritage Auctions, HA.com*)

MAY 8, 1753: The reported birthday of Phillis Wheatley, the first female African poet to be published while a slave in America in 1767. Her *Poems on Various Subjects, Religious and Moral* was published as a book on September 1, 1773.

A two-page letter written and signed by her excelled at $253,000 at Swann Auction Galleries in 2005.

Wheatley's book of poems

Phillis Wheatley

MAY 9, 1671: Thomas Blood and two men stole the Crown Jewels from the Tower of London—but only for a little while. They were captured nearby. For unspecified reasons, King Charles II released Blood from prison without a trial—even though the crown was hammered flat and the scepter sawn in half to make it easier to abscond with them.

Thomas Blood

MAY 10, 1904: Journalist and explorer Henry Morton Stanley (born John Rowlands) died in London. He found Dr. David Livingstone in Africa and became famous for reportedly asking, "Dr. Livingstone, I presume?"

His 1874 book, *How I Found Livingstone*, inscribed, sold for $17,600 at Christie's in 2004. Eight years later, another inscribed copy sold for $30,000, also at Christie's.

Henry Stanley

Dr. Livingstone was one of the most famous people in Britain in the 19th century. In 2015, his *Missionary Travels and Researches in South Africa* published in 1857 was auctioned for £3000 by Rogers Jones & Co. in Wales—after being purchased at a car boot (trunk) sale for £1. It was autographed and inscribed by Livingstone to a friend.

David Livingstone

MAY 11, 1811: Siamese twins Chang and Eng Bunker were born in Thailand. Exhibited around the world, they became wealthy and settled in North Carolina. Each married, and the two fathered a total of twenty-one children. Eng died a few hours after his brother passed, even though they were only conjoined by their liver and cartilage.

A carte de visite of Chan and Eng and two of their sons made $411 in 2012 at Cowan's Auction.

Eng and Chang *(Photo courtesy of Wellcome Images, a website operated by Wellcome Trust)*

MAY 12, 1820: Englishwoman Florence Nightingale, the "Lady of the Lamp," was born in her namesake city of Florence, Italy. She saved countless lives through nursing and improving hygiene, reducing the death rate in hospitals during the Crimean War from forty-two percent to two percent (Historic-UK.com).

(Continued on the next page.)

A 150-year-old brass desk lamp that belonged to Florence Nightingale sold in 2015 for £17,000 at Hanson's Auctioneers in Derbyshire, UK.

Florence Nightingale

MAY 13, 1914: Joe Louis Barrow, the "Brown Bomber," was born in rural Alabama. Of his sixty-nine professional fights, he won sixty-six by knockout or TKO and was World Heavyweight Champion for twelve straight years (boxrec.com).

A Joe Louis Soda Punch metal sign, 14 x 10 inches, sold for $275 on eBay in 2016. A pair of 1940s Joe Louis fight-worn purple satin trunks went for $15,535 in 2009 at Heritage Auctions.

Louis' trunks (*Photo courtesy of Heritage Auctions, HA.com*)

Joe Louis

Joe Louis Soda Punch sign (*Photo courtesy of Dr. Randy B. Hayward*)

MAY 14, 1804: Lewis and Clark embark on their historic journey of exploration from St. Louis, Missouri.

In 2012, Heritage Auctions sold an 1809 land indenture document signed by Meriwether Lewis and William Clark, reportedly the only known document in private hands signed by both, for $110,000. An 1814 book created from the journals of Lewis and Clark by Paul Allen titled, *History of the Expedition under the Command of Captains Lewis and Clark*, gaveled at Sotheby's for $218,500 in 2012.

Meriwether Lewis

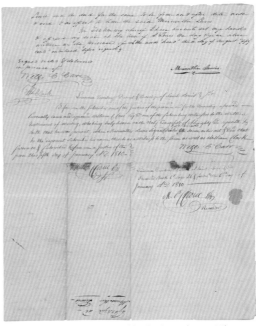

1809 land indenture signed by both explorers (*Photo courtesy of Heritage Auctions, HA.com*)

William Clark

MAY 15, 1856: L. Frank Baum was born. He wrote fourteen novels about Oz, including *The Wonderful Wizard of Oz*; other authors have written dozens more since his passing.

A 1900 edition of the book

L. Frank Baum

In 2013, Bonhams auctioned a first edition, first issue of the book for $87,500; it was one of two known to be signed and inscribed by Baum and the illustrator, William Wallace Denslow.

MAY 16, 1985: Margaret Hamilton passed away, but not by melting. She was best known for the character she played in *The Wonderful Wizard of Oz*—the Wicked Witch of the West. Hamilton was a Sunday School teacher at one time and loved children. She was concerned about how her performance may have affected them.

In the movie, she was burned on her face and hand in the fire-and-smoke scene when she left Munchkinland. Her stunt double was also burned in a scene. Hamilton was much more than her Witch character; she had 121 screen credits over her career (IMDb.com).

Margaret Hamilton

The Wicked Witch of the West's iconic hat from the Pugliese's Pop Culture Collection flew off for $208,250 in 2011 at Guernsey's (www.antiquesandthearts.com, 5/6/08).

The Wicked Witch of the West's hat (*Photo courtesy of Guernsey's*)

MAY 16: Birthdays today: Wladziu Valentino Liberace, 1919, and Pierce Brosnan, 1953. Known for his mastery of the piano and his flamboyant style, one of Liberace's custom pianos with mirrored tiles, a Baldwin Model L grand, sold for $42,500 in 1988 at Christie's (NYT.com, 4/11/1988).

MAY 17, 1620: A great day for youngsters—the first record of a merry-go-round; it was at a fair in Turkey (roughdaily.com). The highest price paid to date for a carved carousel animal was not for a horse ($121,000 at Guernsey's, 1989), but a St. Bernard for $172,000 in 1993 (nytimes.com, 7/3/94 and carouselhistory.com).

MAY 18 1897: Frank Capra was born in Sicily. Writer/director of more than fifty movies, he is known for: *It's A Wonderful Life, Arsenic and Old Lace, Mr. Deeds Goes to Town,* and *Mr. Smith Goes to Washington* (IMDb.com). *It's A Wonderful Life* initially lost money, but it was Jimmy Stewart's favorite movie—and eventually one of America's (bizjournal.com, 12/10/2010).

Frank Capra's Golden Globe for Outstanding Director of 1946 for that movie hammered for $60,000 at Bonhams in 2015.

Frank Capra

Donna Reed, Jimmy Stewart, and Karolyn "Zuzu" Grimes in *It's a Wonderful Life*

MAY 19, 1962: Marilyn Monroe sang "Happy Birthday, Mr. President" to President Kennedy (ten days before his birthday on the 29th). The dress she wore then sold for an eye-popping $4.8 million at Julien's Auctions in 2016.

Marilyn Monroe singing for the President

MAY 19, 1777: Button Gwinnett died in a duel not long after signing the Declaration of Independence as a representative from Georgia.

In 2010, one of his rare signatures sold for $722,500 at Sotheby's. Others have sold for less.

Button Gwinnett

MAY 20, 1908: Movie star and WWII-medaled veteran Jimmy Stewart was born in Indiana, Pennsylvania. AFI's 50 Greatest American Screen Legends listed him as #3 behind Humphrey Bogart #1 and Cary Grant #2 (afi.com).

Stewart rose from private to colonel during the war and flew bombing missions into Germany. He received an Oscar for *Philadelphia Story* (IMDb.com).

In 2006, Bonhams auctioned a sketch of Harvey the Invisible Rabbit drawn by

Jimmy Stewart receiving the Croix de Guerre medal

JAMES STEWART
KIM NOVAK
IN ALFRED HITCHCOCK'S
MASTERPIECE
'VERTIGO'

Stewart and signed by "both" and Stewart's signed photo for $1,195. In 2006, a three sheet movie poster for *Vertigo* (1958) fell for $7,475, and in 2007, a one sheet *Mr. Smith Goes to Washington* (1939) left for $15,535, both at Heritage Auctions.

Vertigo (Photo courtesy of Heritage Auctions, HA.com)

MAY 21, 2016: Julien's Auctions sold Elvis' Gibson Dove guitar for $334,000 and Michael Jackson's Beat It jacket from the History Tour for $256,000.

MAY 22, 1859: Sir Arthur Conan Doyle was born, the creator of Sherlock Holmes, probably the most reproduced character in movies and on TV. IMDb.com lists 150+ movies, TV series, video games, movie shorts, and videos of Sherlock Holmes.

In 2004, Christie's sold for £948,545 a previously unknown archive of 3,000 of Doyle's letters, notes, and manuscripts—including drafts of his first Holmes novel, *A Study in Scarlett*. The cache was found in an attorney's office, left there for forty years.

Sir Arthur Conan Doyle

MAY 23, 1934: Twentysomethings Bonnie Parker and Clyde Barrow were shot dozens of times by police outside Sailes, Louisiana. The two were responsible for at least thirteen murders and an untold number of robberies (of banks, stores, and gas stations), burglaries, auto thefts, and kidnappings.

In 2012, Bonnie's Detective Special .38 hit $264,000 and Clyde's Colt .45 brought $240,000 at RR Auction.

Clyde's .45 and Bonnie's .38 (*Photo courtesy of RRAuction.com*)

Bonnie and Clyde

MAY 24: Birthdays of Queen Victoria, 1819, and George Nakashima, 1905. Nakashima was held in a Japanese Relocation Camp in Idaho for a period during WWII.

A c. 1980 Conoid Bench of American black walnut he made sold at Sotheby's for $25,000 on June 9, 2015. In December, another went for $62,500.

George Nakashima in his workshop (*Photo courtesy of Nakashima Foundation for Peace, nakashimapeacefoundation.org*)

A Nakashima Conoid bench (*Photo courtesy of Sotheby's*)

MAY 25, 1977: The first *Star Wars* movie, Episode IV, debuted. On a budget of $11 million, it made $786+ million worldwide—and that was just at the box office (the-numbers.com). Collecting Star Wars figures has now reached respectability. Sotheby's held an auction in 2015 of 600 figures and other items from the collection of Billionaire Boys Club founder NIGO. The sale yielded $502,000.

MAY 26, 1907: Marion Michael Morrison, aka John Wayne, was born in Iowa. *The Telegraph* reported in 2004 that Stalin loved cowboy movies but ordered the assassination of John Wayne for being an extreme anti-communist. The hit men were unsuccessful, and in 1958, Khrushchev met Wayne, telling him Stalin was crazy, and his order had been rescinded (telegraph.co.uk, 6/4/04).

In 2011, 700+ articles of John Wayne's memorabilia rocketed to $5.3+ million at Heritage Auctions, including: his beret from *The Green Berets*, $179,250; his Golden Globe for *True Grit*, $143,400, and eyepatch, $47,800; and his signature cowboy hat, $119,500.

John Wayne's cowboy hat
(Photo courtesy of Heritage Auctions, HA.com)

John Wayne

His Golden Globe for True Grit (Photo courtesy of Heritage Auctions, HA.com)

John Wayne's beret (Photo courtesy of Heritage Auctions, HA.com)

MAY 27, 1837: The legendary James Butler "Wild Bill" Hickok was born in Troy Grove, Illinois. The Smith & Wesson Model No.2 revolver in his possession when "Crooked Nose Jack" McCall shot him in the back of the head on Aug. 2, 1876 failed to reach the reserve price at Bonhams in 2013; the last bid was $220,000 (reuters.com, 11/18/13).

McCall was at first acquitted of murder and then later rearrested, found guilty, and hanged. What about double jeopardy? A federal court ruled the Deadwood court was not legally constituted and had no jurisdiction, so McCall could be tried again.

"Wild Bill" Hickok

MAY 28, 1908: Ian Fleming, the author of the book *Chitty-Chitty-Bang-Bang: The Magical Car*, was born in London. He also created Mr. Kiss Kiss Bang Bang, James Bond ("Mr. Kiss Kiss Bang Bang" was the theme song from *Thunderball*). With a total of twenty-six movies (at the moment), ten actors have played Bond (evert.meulie.net). Undoubtedly, more are on the way; 007 has raked in $7 billion (the-numbers.com).

Ian Fleming

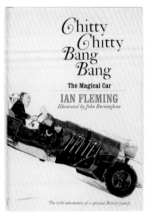

Ian Fleming's book *Chitty-Chitty-Bang-Bang* (Photo courtesy of Heritage Auctions, HA.com)

In 2004, Sotheby's sold a signed and inscribed first edition of the book *Moonraker* for $102,000 (literary007.com). A copy of his 1964 first edition of *Chitty-Chitty-Bang-Bang* went for $337.50 in 2014 at Heritage Auctions.

MAY 29, 1903: Bob Hope made his birth appearance in England. He had a million jokes: "I grew up with six brothers. That's how I learned how to dance—waiting for the bathroom."

A Johnny Carson Friars Club Roast program, hardcover and signed by Bob Hope on the cover and by George Burns, Buddy Hackett, Jimmy Stewart, and Carroll O'Connor, gaveled at Julien's in 2008 for $10,560.

Bob Hope

MAY 30, 1640: Peter Paul Rubens, the Flemish baroque masterpiece creator, passed away this day. Fortunately, he was a prolific painter, because about two dozen of his masterpieces have been lost in fires, in war, and at sea.

Rubens' *Massacre of the Innocents* mastered $76,730,703 on July 10, 2002. Also, his *Portrait of a Gentleman, Half-Length, Wearing Black* fetched $5,273,190 in 2013, both at Sotheby's.

Peter Paul Rubens' self-portrait

The Massacre of the Innocents

Portrait of a Gentleman

MAY 31: Clint Eastwood, 1930, and Walt Whitman, 1819, were born.

A first edition of *Leaves of Grass* printed for Whitman was auctioned for $305,000 in 2014 at Christie's. Clint Eastwood's Colt .44 Walker used in the movie *The Outlaw Josey Wales* was auctioned at Profiles in History for $35,000 in 2010.

Walt Whitman

The "Man with No Name" in *A Fistful of Dollars*

JUNE

JUNE 1, 1938: Superman arrived on Earth in *Action Comics #1*, thanks to Jerry Siegel and Joe Shuster. The cover featured the Man of Steel hefting a green car of steel on the cover. A 9.0-graded copy flew off eBay for $3.2 million in 2014. In 2013, an *Action Comics #1* Billy Wright pedigree CGC GD/VG 3.0 made $388,375 at Heritage Auctions.

Action Comics #1 sold at Heritage Auctions (Photo courtesy of Heritage Auctions, HA. com)

JUNE 1, 1926: The birthday of Norma Jean Mortenson/Marilyn Monroe (See also June 18 and June 27). Marilyn Monroe's personal fawn-colored overcoat sold for $175,000 at Julien's Live in 2014. Her personal makeup case sold at Christie's in 1999 for $266,500 (therichest.com, 02/19/14).

Marilyn Monroe with Arthur Miller, Laurence Olivier, and Vivien Leigh

JUNE 2, 1953: Queen Elizabeth II's coronation in Westminster Abbey generated ad infinitum memorabilia commemorating the event, including cups, plates, photos, books, trinket boxes, medals, etc. that sell for modest amounts.

The Coronation photo of
Queen Elizabeth II and
Prince Phillip

JUNE 3, 2011: Marshal Matt Dillon rode off into the sunset. James Arness passed away at home at the age of eighty-eight. Best known for his twenty seasons on TV's *Gunsmoke*, he also acted in films, including *The Thing From Another World* (he was the Thing). Arness initially turned down the offer for *Gunsmoke*, but John Wayne convinced him to take it (snopes.com).

High Noon Western Americana sold Marshal Dillon's Colt .45 for $59,000 in 2014 (liveauctioneers.com/news, 1/30/14).

James Arness

JUNE 4, 1977: *Poppy Flowers* by Vincent van Gogh was stolen this day from the Mohamed Mahmoud Khalil Museum in Cairo, Egypt—for the first time. It was found and returned in the next decade but stolen again in 2010 from the same museum. The masterpiece is valued at $50+ million.

The still missing
Poppy Flowers

JUNE 5, 1718: Thomas Chippendale was baptized; no record of his exact birth date has been found. Legendary for creating furniture, he was also a marketing genius in publishing his book of designs, *The Gentleman and Cabinet Maker's Director*, which has been copied for centuries. A first edition of it sold for $2,150 in 2015 at Heritage Auctions.

A George II Padouck cabinet-on-stand attributed to Chippendale, 1755–1760, hammered at Christie's in 2008 for $5.32 million.

THE
GENTLEMAN
AND
CABINET-MAKER's
DIRECTOR.
BEING A LARGE
COLLECTION
OF THE MOST
Elegant and Useful Designs of Household Furniture
IN THE
GOTHIC, CHINESE and MODERN TASTE.

Chippendale's book
(Photo courtesy of Heritage
Auctions, HA.com)

JUNE 6, 1868: Royal Navy officer and explorer Captain Robert Falcon Scott was born. In 1912, he and his team made it to the South Pole but were more than a month behind Roald Amundsen, the first to reach it. Unfortunately, Scott and his team all died from exposure, exhaustion, and lack of food on the return trip to their base camp. Even so, "Scott of the Antarctic" became a national hero in Great Britain.

Captain Scott's silk Union Jack taken on his two Antarctic Expeditions, including the last one, rose to $114,929 at Christie's in 2010.

Capt. Scott (*back, middle*) at the South Pole

Capt. Robert Falcon Scott

JUNE 6, 1944: D-Day, the Normandy Invasion by the Greatest Generation. A forty-eight-star flag flown from the Navy Landing Craft Control (LCC) 60 triumphed with $514,000 at Heritage Auctions on June

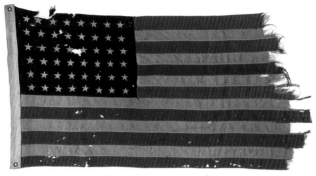

The D-Day Normandy flag (*Photo courtesy of Heritage Auctions, HA.com*)

12, 2016. It was from the personal collection of Lieutenant Howard Vander Beek, the skipper of LCC 60 and the first vessel to deliver troops to Utah Beach—and deliver eighteen more assault waves afterwards. He wrote later, "At some point I looked astern and saw what lay at sea behind us: the greatest armada the world had ever known, the greatest it would ever know. I must have been overwhelmed by the sight as I clung to the rail for a moment to take in the magnitude of that assembled fleet, many great, gray ships majestically poised in their positions; larger numbers of unwieldy landing vessels heaved by the heavy sea; and countless numbers of smaller amphibious craft tossed mercilessly by the waves" (HA.com).

JUNE 7, 1848: Post-impressionist painter Paul Gauguin was born in Paris. His 1892 *When Will You Marry?* depicting two Tahitian women sold in a private sale in 2015 for about $300 million, it is believed. Gauguin counted Cezanne, Pissarro, and van Gogh as friends or acquaintances.

Paul Gaugin

When Will You Marry?

JUNE 8, 1916: Francis Crick was born near Northampton, England. A discoverer of the structure of DNA with James Watson and Maurice Wilkins, all shared a Nobel Prize in 1962.

Crick's Nobel Prize received a bid of $2,270,500 in April 2013 at Heritage Auctions. A year later, Watson's Nobel hit $4.75 million at Christie's; his five-page Nobel banquet speech sold for $365,000 at the same auction.

Their discovery was greatly aided by the work of Rosalind Franklin who died of cancer and pneumonia before the three won the Nobel Prize, which can only be given to the living. Had she survived, she could well have been a Nobel Laureate, too.

Crick's Nobel Prize (*Photo courtesy of Heritage Auctions, HA.com*)

Francis Crick

JUNE 9: The first appearances of: Cole Porter, 1891 ("Night and Day," "I've Got You Under My Skin"); guitar great Lester William Polsfuss (Les Paul), 1915; and Donald Duck, 1934 in *The Wise Little Hen*. A 1954 Gibson Les Paul Custom Black Beauty once

Cole Porter

Les Paul

owned by Paul sold at Guernsey's for $343,750 in 2015 (gizmag.com, 11/4/15). He is the only person that is in the Rock and Roll Hall of Fame and the Inventor's Hall of Fame; he invented the solid body electric guitar (lespaulfoundation.org).

You may not be impressed with his duck speech, but his collectibles are another story. Some original art of Donald Duck sells for six figures, and some art, comic books, and comic strips are in five figures. In 2011, a Carl Barks-drawn *Red Sails in the Sunset* Donald Duck original art painting from 1974 cruised to $113,525 at Heritage Auctions. Have a little more respect for D. Duck now?

Donald in *Red Sails in the Sunset* (Photo courtesy of Heritage Auctions, HA.com)

JUNE 10, 1895: The first African American to win an Academy Award, Hattie McDaniel, was born in Wichita, Kansas. She won Best Supporting Actress for *Gone With The Wind*. She has two stars on the Hollywood Walk of Fame—one for her work in radio and the other in film. A presentation copy of the *GWTW* script given to her by David O. Selznick and signed by him auctioned for $18,300 at Bonhams in 2010.

Hattie McDaniel

JUNE 10, 1988: Prolific western novel author Louis L'Amour passed away in Los Angeles. He wrote more than one hundred novels, and some were made into movies.

An inscribed and signed 1939 first edition of his *Smoke From This Altar* sold for $597 at Heritage Auctions in 2007.

JUNE 11, 1770: Captain James Cook discovered the Great Barrier Reef when his ship *Endeavor* ran aground on it. Cook voyaged far from his home in England to New Zealand, Australia, and to Hawaii where he perished.

In 2003, a gold-mounted hardwood walking cane made from the spear that killed Captain Cook on Feb. 14, 1779 (kept by an officer on the *Endeavor*) was sold for £150,750 at Lyon & Turnbull. It was engraved with: "From Adml. C.B.H. Ross C.B. To Admiral Sir David Milne G.C.B. Made of the spear which killed Captn. Cook R.N." Also, Cook's pistol made $227,100 at Leski Auctions in Australia in 2013.

Capt. Cook's pistol (*Photo courtesy of Mossgreen, mossgreen.com.au*)

The spear made into a cane (*Photo courtesy of Lyon & Turnbull*)

Capt. James Cook

The Death of Captain James Cook, February 14, 1779, by Johan Zoffany, c. 1795

JUNE 11, 1982: *E.T. the Extra-Terrestrial* flew across the night sky at its release and was the top-grossing film of 1982 with $792.8 million worldwide (the-numbers. com). It won four Academy Awards (IMDb.com).

An urban legend about Atari dumping *E.T. the Extra-Terrestrial* video games and others in a landfill in New Mexico was proven to actually be true in 2014 with an excavation. About 1,300 games were unearthed, including: *Yars' Revenge, Star Raiders, Pac-Man, Space Invaders, Defender,* and *Warlords,* along with *E.T.* The *Alamogordo Daily News* (6/20/15) reported the city planned to sell about 900 of the games in rounds on eBay. Sales (at the time of this writing) have totaled $108,000+ with more than $1,500 being the highest paid for an *E.T.*—which has been called the worst video game ever.

The Atari excavation (*Photo courtesy of Taylorhatmaker*)

JUNE 12, 1929: Anne Frank's birthday. Her diary is on display at the Anne Frank Museum in Amsterdam with her other diaries and manuscripts.

A group of letters from Anne and her sister Margot to pen-pals in America sold for $165,000 in 1988 at Swann Auction Galleries. A signed copy of Anne Frank's *Grimm's*

Anne Frank in school

(Continued on the next page.)

Fairy Tales (*Aus Grimms Märchen*) left behind and later found in a second-hand shop gaveled for $62,500 on May 5, 2016 at Swann's Auction Galleries.

Anne Frank's *Grimm's Fairy Tales*, the cover, and the signed title page (*Photos courtesy of Swann Auction Galleries*)

JUNE 12, 1963: *Cleopatra*, the six-hour-movie-cut-down-to-four-hours starring Elizabeth Taylor and Richard Burton, debuted. It only earned $26 million that year, with a budget of $44 million (xfinity.com). At this time, it is at $57 million worldwide (the-numbers.com). It won four Oscars (IMDb.com). Elizabeth Taylor's/Cleopatra's gold-painted leather Phoenix cape gaveled at $59,375 at Heritage Auctions in 2012.

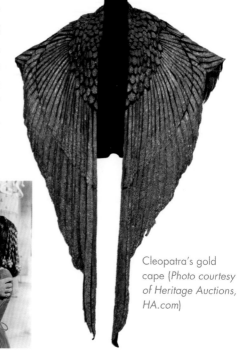

Richard Burton and Elizabeth Taylor in *Cleopatra*

Cleopatra's gold cape (*Photo courtesy of Heritage Auctions, HA.com*)

JUNE 13, 2010: Little Orphan Annie was canceled in the comic strips after eighty-six years. Rather than exiting singing "Tomorrow," Annie left her comic strip in a cliffhanger: kidnapped by "The Butcher of the Balkans" while Daddy Warbucks thinks she's dead (comicsalliance.com). In 2011, a hardcover *Little Orphan Annie #1* of early comic strips valued at $200 went for just $30 at Heritage Auctions. Poor Annie.

Little Orphan Annie #1 (Photo courtesy of Heritage Auctions, HA.com)

JUNE 13, 1831: The man on whose shoulders Einstein said he stood, James Clerk Maxwell, was born in Scotland. Maxwell discovered the relationship of electricity and magnetism and the principle that light is an electromagnetic wave. He also created the first color photograph and proved that Saturn's rings are made of particles (famousscientists.org).

James Clerk Maxwell

In 2013, Christie's sold his 1873 *A Treatise on Electricity and Magnetism* for $22,860.

JUNE 14, 1801: Revolutionary War general and traitor Benedict Arnold died in London. Foiled in his plan to hand over West Point, NY, to the British, Arnold was commissioned a brigadier general in the Redcoat army and given a pension and a lump sum payment worth $600,000 today. He actually led British raids in Virginia and Connecticut.

Benedict Arnold

A signed letter from him dated May 6, 1776, before his defection, hammered for $20,546 at RR Auction in 2013. Most of his signed documents sell for a few thousand dollars.

JUNE 14, 1811: Birthday of Harriet Beecher Stowe, author of *Uncle Tom's Cabin*. First editions can usually be found for a few hundred dollars.

Harriet Beecher Stowe

JUNE 15, 1937: Waylon Jennings was born and had hits like "Mamas Don't Let Your Babies Grow Up to Be Cowboys" and "Good Hearted Woman" ("in love with a good timin' man"). He is acknowledged as one of country music's greats.

In 2014, Guernsey's sold Waylon Jennings' 1958 Ariel Cyclone motorcycle (that once belonged to his friend Buddy Holly) for $457,500.

In 1959, Waylon gave us his seat on a plane for "The Big Bopper" J.P. Richardson during a music tour. Also on the group's plane was Richie Valens and Buddy Holly. It crashed, taking all three.

Waylon Jennings in 1965

JUNE 16, 1829: The great Apache leader Geronimo was born. His Model 1870 Springfield rifle hammered for $99,450 at Bonhams & Butterfields in 2007.

Geronimo holding his Springfield

JUNE 16, 1890: Stan Laurel of Laurel and Hardy fame was born in Lancashire, England. Born Arthur Stanley Jefferson, Laurel made 180+ movies, mostly shorts (IMDb.com). He once said, "If any of you cry at my funeral, I'll never speak to you again!" (brainyquote.com). In 2013, his gag journal sold for $3,520 at Julien's Auctions.

Stan Laurel

JUNE 17, 2014: The British Guiana one cent magenta stamp spiked at $9.4 million at Sotheby's, the highest price paid to date for a stamp.

The British Guiana
1 cent magenta stamp

JUNE 17, 1917: Singer and actor Dino Crocetti, aka Dean Martin, was born in Ohio. In 2008, Julien's Live auctioned one of his tuxedos, two bow ties, and a signed and inscribed photo for $20,000.

JUNE 18, 2011: Marilyn Monroe's white Subway Dress from *The Seven Year Itch* peaked at $5.6 million at Profiles in History, the most paid to date for a Hollywood dress. The scene on a street had to be reshot on a sound stage due to noise from a large crowd of reporters and onlookers (biography.com, 9/15/14). The dress was part of a collection owned by actress Debbie Reynolds.

The Subway Dress

JUNE 19: Debuting this day were: the Tasmanian Devil in *Devil May Hare*, 1954; the Garfield cartoon strip, 1978; and Guy Lombardo, 1902. A Tasmanian Devil 3.5 x 5-inch production cel from *Dr. Devil and Mr. Hare* (1964) spun up $1,553 in 2013 at Heritage Auctions.

The intro of Taz (*Photo courtesy of Heritage Auctions, HA.com*)

JUNE 20: The birthdays of: actor Errol Flynn, 1909; guitarist Chet Atkins, 1924; Medal of Honor recipient and actor Audie Murphy, 1925; and Beach Boy Brian Wilson, 1942. *Toast of the Town*, later called *The Ed Sullivan Show*, debuted in 1948 and ran for twenty-three years. *Jaws* swam into history in 1975, eventually earning $470+ million. Also this day in 1893, after 1.5 hours of deliberation, a jury found Lizzie Borden innocent of the murders of her parents. A 1 x .75-inch fragment from a brick in the Borden's chimney sold for $203 in 2008 at Heritage Auctions.

Trial of Lizzie Borden, depicted in Frank Leslie's *Illustrated Weekly*

Audie Murphy

Lizzie Borden

Errol Flynn

JUNE 21, 1859: The birthday of one of the greatest African-American painters of the 19th century, Henry Ossawa Tanner. Born in Pittsburg, he moved to France where he became internationally known for his religious paintings. His work is held by museums across the country, including the Smithsonian and in Paris. In 2003, his *Nicodemus Coming to Christ* sold for $541,000 at Christie's.

Henry Ossawa Tanner

Tanner's *The Annunciation*, 1898, in the Philadelphia Museum of Art

JUNE 22, 1965: David O. Selznick passed away. His collection documenting his career was bequeathed to the Harry Ransom Center at the University of Texas in Austin; it fills more than 5,000 boxes and includes half a million photos (hrc.utexas.edu). He produced eighty-seven movies, including *Gone With The Wind* and *King Kong* with Fay Wray (IMDb.com).

David O. Selznick

JUNE 22, 1969: The star Judy Garland (Frances Ethel Gumm) passed away. Her blue-and-white gingham pinafore "Dorothy" dress from *The Wizard of Oz* conjured up $1,565,000 at Bonhams in 2015.

Judy Garland

Dorothy in her gingham dress

JUNE 23, 1912: Birth of English mathematical wizard Alan M. Turing who led the team that cracked the German's Enigma code in WWII. A 3-motor Enigma I Enciphering Machine, 1944, auctioned for $269,000 at Bonhams in 2015, and a 1953 letter signed by Turing was taken for $136,122 at RR Auction in 2016.

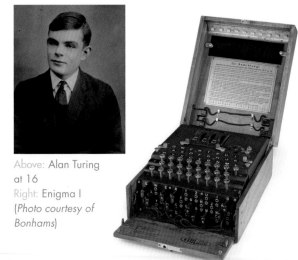

Above: Alan Turing at 16
Right: Enigma I
(Photo courtesy of Bonhams)

JUNE 24, 1895: "The Manassa Mauler" Jack Dempsey was born. Of his eighty-three fights, he had sixty-five wins, fifty-one by knockout. In WWII, Dempsey earned the rank of commander and took part in the Okinawa invasion on board the USS *Arthur Middleton*, a transport ship.

Dempsey's 1926 Heavyweight World Championship belt and a photo of him receiving it hit $44,812 at Heritage Auction in 2005.

Jack Dempsey

JUNE 25, 1903: Eric Arthur Blair, aka George Orwell, was born in India. Author of *Animal Farm* and *1984*, Gorringes in the U.K. sold a signed 1933 first edition of his first full-length work, *Down and Out in Paris and London*, for £86,000 in 2010. He died at forty-six of tuberculosis.

George Orwell

JUNE 25, 2011: A tintype photo of Billy the Kid hammered for $2.3 million at Brian Lebel's Old West Auction. This photo gave rise to the myth that he was a left-handed gun because as a tintype, the image was flipped (aboutbillythekid.com).

Billy the Kid
tintype

JUNE 25, 2011: One of Michael Jackson's two black and red leather jackets worn in *Thriller* sold for $1.8 million at Julien's Auction.

JUNE 26 AND 27, 1906:

The first international Grand Prix was run outside Le Mans, France, on tarred dirt roads closed to the public. The course was about sixty-four miles long, and each driver was required

Ferenc Szisz

Szisz crossing the finish line

to run six laps each day. The tar heated up under those speeding tires, which flung it into the faces of drivers. Ferenc Szisz won the first French Grand Prix for the Renault Team. In 2011, the 1970 Porsche 911S Steve McQueen drove in the movie *Le Mans* sped off for $1,375,000 at RM Auction/Sothebys.

JUNE 27, 2015: Marilyn Monroe's grave marker from the Westwood Village Memorial Park Cemetery in Los Angeles sold for $212,500 at Julien's Auctions.

(*Photo courtesy of Julien's Auctions*)

JUNE 28, 1491: Henry VIII was born.

In 1965, Herman's Hermits either immortalized or embarrassed him with "I'm Henry the Eighth, I Am," which made it to No. 1 on Billboard's Top 100. However, it was not original with Herman or his Hermits; the song was written in 1910 by Fred Murray and R. P. Weston. In 2011, NateD-Sanders.com auctioned a Henry VIII-signed document from the 16th century for $49,374.

Henry VIII,
c. 1530-1535

JUNE 28, 2012: De-

lightful memorabilia from the movie *Willy Wonka and The Chocolate Factory* (1979) sold at Profiles in History: Veruca Salt's Everlasting Gobstopper

Willy Wonka's hat (*Photo courtesy of Profiles in History*)

Veruca's Everlasting Gobstopper (*Photo courtesy of Profiles in History*)

(one of only two known to exist), $40,000; Willy Wonka's outfit including the purple velvet coat, slacks, white shirt, purple and violet lamé vest, and floral satin tie, $60,000; Willy Wonka's brown felt tophat sold separately for $27,500; and an Oompa Loompa costume with a rust-colored shirt and striped collar and cuffs, white jodhpurs, leather slippers with pom-poms, and a green wig for $25,000. (Prices do not include buyer's premium.)

JUNE 29: No good news today. Movie star Jayne Mansfield was killed in an auto accident in 1967. Another movie star, Lana Turner, passed away in 1995, and popular singer and actress (with Bing Crosby in *White Christmas*) Rosemary Clooney died in 2002. In 2012, a pale yellow gown made for Jayne Mansfield by Emeson's was auctioned for $3,200 in 2012 at Julien's Live.

Jayne Mansfield   Lana Turner   Rosemary Clooney

JUNE 30, 1953: The first Corvette rolled off the line. However, it only had a six-cylinder engine (history.com) and was not yet the muscle car it was destined to become. Only 300 were made.

1953 Corvette

The highest auction amount paid for a Corvette was $3.85 million for a 1967 Chevrolet Corvette L88 Coupe sold by Barrett-Jackson in 2014 (cnbc.com, 1/21/14).

JULY

JULY 1: Born today were Blues Brother and ghostbuster Dan Akroyd, 1952, and Carl Lewis, winner of ten Olympic medals, 1961. Michael (Eugene Maurice Orowitz) Landon passed away in 1991 from pancreatic cancer at the age of fifty-four. *Bonanza*, *Little House on the Prairie*, and *Highway to Heaven* were his most popular TV shows. His Colt .38 from *Bonanza* sold for $12,000 in 2011 at Profiles in History.

Michael Landon

JULY 2, 1937: NASCAR legend Richard Petty was born. In 2015, he donated a customized 2015 Ford Mustang GT to be auctioned with proceeds going to Paralyzed Veterans of America. It sold for $330,000 at Mecum Auctions and then was immediately donated back to sell again for $205,000 (mecum.com, 9/23/15).

Richard Petty and his donated 2015 Ford Mustang GT (*Photo courtesy of Mecum Auctions*)

JULY 3, 1908: The passing of Joel Chandler Harris, aka Uncle Remus, at the age of fifty-nine. A cast iron Uncle Remus mechanical bank, 5.75 inches long and manufactured by Kyser & Rex, yielded $22,000 at Morphy Auctions in 2012.

Joel Chandler Harris in 1873

Uncle Remus bank (*Photo courtesy of Morphy Auctions*)

JULY 3, 1985: *Back To The Future* debuted and thrilled the world. It was a labor of love for Michael J. Fox because his TV series *Family Ties* was shot during the day, and his part in the movie was filmed at night and on weekends (IMDb.com). Marty's "future" 2015 Nike Mags self-lacing shoes from *Back to the Future II* sold for $84,000 in 2015 at Profiles in History. A *Back to the Future* one sheet movie poster, 27 x 41 inches, flew off for $597.50 in 2015 at Heritage Auctions.

(Photo courtesy of Heritage Auctions, HA.com)

JULY 4, 1939: Lou Gehrig gave his "Luckiest Man on the Face of the Earth" speech in Yankee Stadium. In part, he said: "Fans, for the past two weeks you have been reading about the bad break I got. Yet today, I consider myself the luckiest man on the face of the earth. I have been in ballparks for seventeen years and have never received anything but kindness and encouragement from you fans." He was forced to retire because of ALS, the disease that now bears his name. Lou Gehrig, "The Iron Horse," set the record with 2,130 consecutive games played. That lasted until Cal Ripken, Jr.'s 2,632. In August

Lou Gehrig

2015, at loveofthegameauctions.com, a Gehrig bat sold for $436,970—many times higher than normal because a photo showed Gehrig holding it.

JULY 5, 1801: Rear-Admiral David G. Farragut was born. In the Battle of Mobile Bay (that he won) during the Civil War, he famously commanded, "Damn the torpedoes! Full speed ahead!" Farragut's U.S.N. autographed manuscript and hand-drawn plan for the Battle of New Orleans sold for $44,000 at Christie's in 1992.

Admiral
Farragut

JULY 5, 2002: Baseball legend Ted Williams passed away. In April 2012, Hunt Auctions sold his memorabilia for $3.5 million. His 1949 American League Most Valuable Player Award plaque, .344 batting average, hit $260,000, and his 1957 Babe Ruth Sultan of Swat Award, earned with a batting average of .388, rose to $200,000 (without 15% buyer's premium).

Ted Williams

Williams' Sultan of Swat
Crown (*Photo courtesy of
Hunt Auctions*)

His 1949 MVP plaque
(*Photo courtesy of Hunt
Auctions*)

JULY 6: Birthdays galore: Bill "Rock Around the Clock" Haley, 1925; *Psycho* actress Janet Leigh, 1927; and "Yo, Adrian" Sylvester Stallone, 1946. In 2015, Heritage Auctions had a hit selling Stallone's memorabilia for $3+ million. His *Rocky* jacket

(Continued on the next page.)

from the first movie was the top lot at $149,000, and his *Rambo* canvas poncho with faux bullet holes made $60,000.

Sylvester Stallone   Rocky's jacket (*Photo courtesy*   The Rambo poncho (*Photo courtesy*
of Heritage Auctions, HA.com)   *of Heritage Auctions, HA.com*)

JULY 7, 1550: Chocolate first appeared in Europe as a drink. A c. 1760 silver chocolate pot by Thomas Hammersley sold for $144,000 at Sotheby's in 2005. Birthdays today: artist Marc Chagall, 1887; Leroy "Satchel" Paige, 1906 (see also Feb. 9); sci-fi writer Robert Heinlein, 1907; and Beatle Ringo Starr, 1940. In 2015 at Julien's Auctions, The Collection of Ringo Starr and Barbara Bach reached almost $10 million. A 1964 Rose-Morris Rickenbacker, model 1996 guitar given to Ringo by John Lennon, excelled at $910,000.

JULY 8, 1947: "RAAF Captures Flying Saucer on Ranch" reported the *Roswell Daily Record.* And so it began . . . and is yet to be resolved to the satisfaction of many. In 2008, $78,000 was paid at Profiles in History for the flying saucer model used in *Forbidden Planet.* The eighty-two-inch diameter model "United Planets Cruiser C-57D" had been stored in a garage for many years (herocomplex.latimes.com, 12/9/08).

A *Forbidden Planet* (1956) 30 x 40-inch movie poster—one of only six known to exist—auctioned for $10,157 in 2012 at Heritage Auctions.

(*Photo courtesy of Heritage Auctions, HA.com*)

JULY 8, 1999: The third man to walk on the moon, Apollo 12 Commander Charles "Pete" Conrad, was killed in a motorcycle accident at the age of sixty-nine. His tie tack flown in the Apollo 12 Lunar Module sold for $1,792.50 in 2012 at Heritage Auctions.

Pete Conrad

Conrad's tie tack (*Photo courtesy of Heritage Auctions, HA.com*)

Conrad examining the unmanned *Surveyor III* spacecraft with Lunar Module *Intrepid* in the background.

JULY 9: Sewing machine inventor Elias Howe's birthday in 1819 and inventive actor Tom Hanks in 1956. In 2016, Lelands. com auctioned Tom Hanks' complete Rockford Peaches uniform from *A League of Their Own* for $13,343.

Tom Hanks' complete Rockford Peaches uniform (*Photo courtesy of Lelands.com*)

JULY 10, 1834: The birthday of James Whistler who made his mother Anna Matilda McNeill Whistler famous with his painting, *Arrangement in Grey and Black No.1,*

Arrangement in Grey and Black No. 1

Arrangement in Grey and Black No. 2

aka *Whistler's Mother.* It resides in the Musée d'Orsay in Paris. *Arrangement in Grey and Black No.* 2 was not of his father, George Washington Whistler, as one might think, but of Scottish satirist Thomas Carlyle. Doyle New York auctioned Whistler's pastel, *The Palace; white and pink,* of a palazzo in Venice for $650,500 in May 2012.

Whistler's self-portrait

JULY 11, 1920: Yul Brynner, famous for *The King and I* and *The Ten Commandments,* was born. A gold metal bracelet with rectangular bars that he wore as Ramses II sold for $1,654 in 2011 at Christie's.

Brynner in *The King and I*

Martin Luther King Jr., 1963

On this day in 1977, Rev. Martin Luther King, Jr. received the Presidential Medal of Freedom, posthumously.

JULY 12, 2014: A Babe Ruth-signed letter written while a consultant on the set of *The Pride of the Yankees* sold for $9,750 at Goldin's Auction (forbes.com, 7/7/14). The letter was part of a scrapbook of letters from celebrities that had been purchased at an estate sale for $1.

Gary Cooper and Babe Ruth on the set of *The Pride of the Yankees*

JULY 13, 1942: The carpenter-turned-actor Harrison Ford was born. A screen-used bullwhip from *Indiana Jones* made $204,000 at Profiles in History in 2015.

Harrison Ford (*Photo courtesy of Gage Skidmore*)

JULY 13, 1944: The birthday of Erno Rubik, inventor of the Rubik's Cube. Even though it has 519 quintillion possible combinations (that's why it's so hard!), more than 350 million cubes have been sold (nypost.com, 5/20/14). In 2014, a mosaic portrait of Robin Williams made with 600 Rubik's Cubes titled, *Goofball*, sold for $4,450 on eBay. It was created by Pete Fecteau, a Rubik's Cube mosaic artist.

Erno Rubik

JULY 14, 1934: Headline this day on a *New York Times* article: "Ruth's Record of 700 Home Runs Likely to Stand for All Time in Major Leagues." After his 700th home run ball sailed over the right field fence, it was snagged by a young Lenny Bielski who had the privilege of giving it back to the Babe and then watching the rest of the game with him, Lou Gehrig, and the rest of the Yankees. Ruth paid Lenny $20 (about $358 today) for the ball and signed another one for him.

JULY 15, 1779: Birthday of Clement Clarke Moore, author of *A Visit From St. Nicholas*, or *'Twas the Night Before Christmas*. A handwritten and signed copy of it sold for $280,000 in 2006 in a private sale brokered by Heritage Auctions. Three other copies are in museums (hhhistory.com).

Clement Moore

JULY 16: Many births: Roald Amundsen, 1872, the first to the South Pole; "Shoeless" Joe Jackson, 1887 (also see Aug. 7); and actress/dancer Ginger Rogers, 1911. Mary Todd Lincoln passed away on this day in 1882. A signed letter from Amundsen sold in 2015 for $3,125 at Bonhams. In 1928,

Roald Amundsen

The "Shoeless" Joe Jackson photo

while on a rescue mission to the Arctic, Amundsen's plane was lost, and he and the crew were never found.

A 1911 "Shoeless Joe" Jackson-signed photo graded PSA/DNA Mint 9 gaveled for $179,250 in 2015 at Heritage Auctions. It is the only signed and graded photo known of him; Jackson was illiterate so his signatures are rare. He has been called the greatest hitter of the decade. From 1908 to 1920, his batting average was .356 with 1,772 hits.

JULY 17: Erle Stanley Gardner, creator of *Perry Mason* and writer of detective stories was born in 1889. Also this day: the singer/dancer/"gangster"/actor James Cagney was born in 1899. The only known one sheet Style A movie poster of Cagney's *The Public Enemy* (1931) auctioned for $167,300, and his screen-worn suit from *Yankee Doodle Dandy* sold for $11,950, both at Heritage Auctions.

Cagney's *Yankee Doodle Dandy* suit (Photo courtesy of Heritage Auctions, HA.com)

Cagney in *The Public Enemy* (Photo courtesy of Heritage Auctions, HA.com)

JULY 18, 1913: The beloved clown and comedian Richard Bernard "Red" Skelton graced the earth this day. In vaudeville, on TV (*The Red Skelton Show* was on for twenty years), on the radio, in movies, and on the Internet, he won hearts by making us laugh. A prolific painter of clowns, Julien's Live sold his oil painting of a clown in a yellow Nehru jacket for $3,437 in 2009. Also born this day were Nelson Mandela, 1918, and John Glenn, Jr., 1921, the first American to orbit the Earth.

Red Skelton

JULY 18, 1863: The 54th Massachusetts Volunteer Infantry, the Union's first African-American unit, led a valorous attack on Ft. Wagner in South Carolina; more than fifty were killed, including the 54th's commander, Colonel Robert Shaw. In 1900, Sergeant William Harvey Carney of the 54th was awarded the Medal of Honor for his actions in that battle—the first African American to receive it by date of his actions, even though others were awarded it before him. Raynor's Historical Collectible Auction sold an inscribed wooden toothbrush belonging to George Ringgold of the 54th Mass. for $998 in 2006.

Sgt. William Harvey Carney

JULY 19, 1834: The famous painter of ballet dancers, horse races, and women at their *toilette,* Edgar Degas was born this day. He never married. Also a sculptor, his *Petite Danseuse de Quatorze Ans* (Little Dancer of Fourteen Years) auctioned for $24,998,740 at Sotheby's in 2015. This was one of more than twenty bronze casts made from his original wax sculpture.

He was also an early innovator in photography.

Edgar Degas' selfie, c. 1895

Petite Danseuse de Quatorze Ans (Photo courtesy of M.T. Abraham Center)

JULY 20, 1969: A day always to remember, Astronaut Neil Armstrong stepped onto the moon. He was followed later by Buzz Aldrin while Michael Collins orbited the moon. They all received the Presidential Medal of Freedom. A check for $10.50 that Neil Armstrong wrote and signed on the day of the Apollo 11 launch, July 16, 1969, reached $27,350 at RR Auctions in 2009. Buzz Aldrin later wrote in his book,

"One small step . . ."

Magnificent Desolation: The Long Journey Home from the Moon, their computers onboard had only 74kb of memory (dailymail.co.uk, 8/21/09).

JULY 21: Funny thing, actors Don Knotts, 1924, and Robin Williams, 1951, were born on this day. Williams' *Mork from Ork* spacesuit sold for $19,200, and the board game from his movie *Jumanji,* with a letter from the director, brought $52,275 at Profiles in History in 2014.

JULY 22, 1882: The birthday of renowned artist Edward Hopper. In 2013, his *East Wind Over Weehawken* skyrocketed to $40,485,000 at Christie's. Hopper is perhaps

Nighthawks

(Continued on the next page.)

Edward Hopper's self-portrait   *East Wind Over Weehawken*

best known for *Nighthawks*, a painting of people at a cafeteria counter seen through a window at night. It was sold to the Art Institute of Chicago for $3,000 soon after it was completed in 1942 (edwardhopper.net).

JULY 23, 1885: President and General Ulysses S. Grant died at sixty-three. His signed letter to General George Thomas saying he had taken the oath to become a brigadier (one-star) general made $15,000 at Christie's in 2012. Other letters signed by him on common topics sell for much less.

JULY 23, 1962: Jackie Robinson was inducted into the Baseball Hall of Fame, the first African American to enter that hallowed Hall. He was also the first to break the color barrier in baseball in the 20th century. A few other African Americans played for major league teams in the late 1800s, like Moses Fleetwood Walker for the Toledo Blue Stockings (see Oct. 7), before the color barrier completely closed in 1890. Jackie Robinson's Rawlings glove—said to have been used during the last three years of his career, including in his 1955 World Series

Jackie Robinson

win and in the 1956 World Series, his last game—was a hit at $373,002 at Steiner Sports in 2013.

JULY 24, 1897: Amelia Earhart was born. In 1991, a sheet of aluminum believed to be a patch on her plane was found (news.discovery.com, 10/28/14). Goggles she wore in 1932 in her solo flight across the Atlantic—the first woman to do so—were sold for $141,600 in 2009 at Profiles in History.

Amelia Earhart

JULY 25, 1834: Death of the author of *The Rime of the Ancient Mariner*, Samuel Taylor Coleridge. A 1910 bound copy of that work went for $3,500 in 2010 at Christie's.

Samuel Taylor Coleridge

Gustave Doré's engraving highlighting the albatross from *The Rime of the Ancient Mariner*

JULY 25, 1956: The Italian liner *Andrea Doria* sank after a collision with another ship—forty-six lives were lost. A red-and-white life preserver ring from the *Andrea Doria* sold for $7,910 at Philip Weiss Auctions in 2012.

JULY 26, 1856: George Bernard Shaw was born in Dublin, Ireland, the only person to win both the Nobel Prize (1925, Literature) and an Academy Award (*Pygmalion*, 1938; IMDb.com). In 1894, author Aldous L. Huxley was born and once said: "Most human beings have an almost infinite capacity for

George Bernard Shaw   Aldus Huxley

taking things for granted" (brainyquote.com). A 1932 edition of his book, *Brave New World*, with dust jacket, auctioned at Christie's for $1,045 in 2010.

JULY 26, 1928: Film director Stanley Kubrick premiered in life and eventually produced classics: *Spartacus* (1960), which made $60 million worldwide, and *2001: A Space Odyssey* (1968), $68.7 million total (the-numbers.com). In 2015, The Academy of Motion Picture Arts and Sciences purchased *2001*'s model Aries 1B Trans-Lunar Space Shuttle for $344,000 at a Premiere Props auction. Kubrick destroyed most of the props after the movie to prevent their being recycled into other movies (latimes.com, 3/29/15). However, he did not complete-

The Aries 1B (*Photo courtesy of Premiere Props*)

ly destroy HAL (Heuristically programmed ALgorithmic), the murderous master computer on the *Discovery One* spacecraft. Christie's sold one of the front panels that held the HAL 9000's red camera eye for $27,615 in 2010. Also included in the sale was an aluminum key similar to that used by astronaut Dave Bowman to access HAL's memory and shut it down.

JULY 27, 2013: George Everett "Bud" Day passed away. He served as an Air Force pilot in WWII, the Korean War, and Vietnam and is the only known recipient of both the Medal of Honor and the Air Force Cross. In 1969, Colonel Day was shot down twenty miles north of the DMZ in North Vietnam. He was captured, but despite a broken arm and having no boots, he escaped. Being pursued for almost two weeks, he made it to within two miles of a Marine base before being shot and captured again. He spent five years and seven months in North Vietnamese prisons and was tortured and starved. John McCain shared a cell with him at one time. After his release, he was awarded the Medal of Honor for bravery while a prisoner.

Col. Bud Day

It is illegal to sell a Medal of Honor, and doing so can reap a fine of up to $100,000 and a year in prison (stripes.com, 11/11/03). It is illegal to wear, manufacture, or sell any medals authorized by Congress for the armed forces. Of course, this does not apply to other countries, and Medals of Honor have been sold outside the States and found on eBay. One sold there for $213.22 in 2016 from an eBay seller in Germany. Some are fakes and others are genuine "illegal" versions made by previous government contractors (ebay.com, "Fake, Copies of the US Medal of Honor Sold on eBay").

JULY 28, 1929: The birthday of First Lady Jacqueline Bouvier Kennedy Onassis. A signed Jacques Lowe photo of her sold for $1,000 at Heritage Auctions in 2015.

Jacqueline Kennedy, c. 1961–1962 (*Photo courtesy of Heritage Auctions, HA.com*)

JULY 29, 2010: Winston Churchill's false teeth closed on $23,700 at Keys Auction House in Aylsham, U.K. (cnn.com, 7/29/10).

JULY 29, 1982: Harold Sakata passed away at the age of sixty-two. A Hawaiian of Japanese descent, Harold was an Olympic Silver Medalist in weightlifting

Oddjob's deadly hat (*Photo courtesy of Guernsey's*)

Harold "Oddjob" Sakata (*Photo courtesy of jamesbondautographs. blogspot.com*)

at the 1948 Summer Olympics, a professional wrestler and—Oddjob! One of the greatest henchmen in the Bond movies.

Harold was famous for tossing his deadly, slicing hat like a Frisbee. One of the steel-brimmed hats worn by Oddjob (sometimes written "Odd Job") in *Goldfinger* hit $110,000 at Guernsey's in 2008. The other sold at Christie's in 1998 for $104,408.

JULY 30: A 1933 $20 Double Eagle coin designed by Augustus Saint-Gaudens sold for $7.59 million—plus $20 to make it legal tender—at Sotheby's in 2002. Also, the author of *Wuthering Heights,* Emily Bronte, was born this day in 1818.

A Saint-Gaudens $20 Double Eagle

JULY 31, 1965: Joanne Rowling, known as "JK," was born. The chair she sat in while writing *Harry Potter and the Sorcerer's Stone* and *Harry Potter and the Chamber of Secrets* sold at Heritage Auctions on April 6, 2016 for $394,000. She signed the backrest and wrote on the apron of the seat: "I wrote / Harry Potter / while sitting / on this chair."

JK Rowling's writing chair (*Photo courtesy of Heritage Auctions, HA.com*)

AUGUST

AUGUST 1: Born this day were: Francis Scott Key, 1779, the attorney who wrote "The Star Spangled Banner" during the War of 1812; Herman Melville, 1819, author of *Moby Dick*; and cartoonist Tom Wilson, 1931, the "father" of *Ziggy*. In 1944, Anne Frank made her last entry in her diary.

Lyrics of "The Star Spangled Banner" printed in 1814, without the author's name listed, auctioned for $506,500 in 2010 at Christie's. Of the eleven known copies, this was the only one in private hands.

Francis Scott Key

AUGUST 2, 2015: The 1882 Colt revolver belonging to gunfighter, lawman, gambler, and sports reporter Bat Masterson sold for $96,000 at J. Levine Auction. After his gunfighting days, Masterson reported on prizefighting, sports, and other newsy topics for the *New York Morning Telegraph*. He died of a heart attack on October 25, 1921 at his desk . . . with his boots on.

Bat Masterson

Bat's revolver
(Photo courtesy of Tim Nelson and J. Levine Auction)

AUGUST 3: Gordon Scott (*Tarzan, Hercules*) came swinging into life in 1926, along with Martha Stewart, 1941, and Jay North (Dennis the Menace), 1951. Carolyn Jones (Morticia on *The Addams Family*) passed away in 1983. A Gordon Scott photo as Tarzan, 16 x 20 inches and signed, called out $156 in 2002. How many remember that Carolyn Jones starred with Elvis Presley in *King Creole* (1958)? That 27 x 41-inch movie poster sold for $448 in 2007. Both sold at Heritage Auctions.

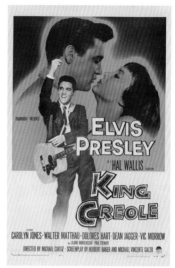

King Creole (Photo courtesy of Heritage Auctions, HA.com)

Gordon Scott as Hercules *(Photo courtesy of Heritage Auctions, HA.com)*

Carolyn Jones in 1953

Carolyn "Morticia" Jones

AUGUST 4, 1901: Trumpeter extraordinaire Louis Armstrong was born. His nickname "Satchmo" was shortened from "satchel mouth," which referred to, well, you know. A #5219 Selmer trumpet owned by Louis Armstrong sold in 2008 for $27,500 at Christie's.

Louis Armstrong

AUGUST 5: Birthdays of actor and director John Huston, 1906 (*The Maltese Falcon, The African Queen,* and *The Misfits*), and Neil Armstrong, 1930. American Bandstand debuted nationally in 1957.

In 2013, Bonham's auctioned the forty-five-lb. lead Maltese Falcon statuette used

John Huston in *Chinatown,* 1972

The $4 million Falcon (*Photo courtesy of Bonhams*)

in the Humphrey Bogart movie for $4,085,000. A resin Falcon used for still photos sold at Guernsey's in 2010 for $305,000 to a group of collectors that included Leonardo DiCaprio.

AUGUST 6, 1911: The Queen of Comedy, Lucille Ball, was born to bring laughter to the world. Known for her red hair, Lucy was naturally a brunette. With four TV series, TV specials, and 100+ movies, Lucy acted almost every year but one between 1933 and 1977 (IMDb.com).

A 1975 photo of her by Cindy Sherman sold for $23,750 at Heritage Auctions in 2013. Other copies have sold for less.

Cindy Sherman's photo of Lucy (*Photo courtesy of Heritage Auctions, HA.com*)

AUGUST 7, 2001: Joseph Jefferson "Shoeless Joe" Jackson's "Black Betsy" bat homered for $577,610 on eBay. His twelve-year career (batting average .356) was cut short by the Black Sox scandal where eight White Sox players were banned from baseball for committing fraud in allowing the Cincinnati Reds to win the 1919 World Series. All were acquitted in court but banned nonetheless.

"Shoeless" Joe Jackson

AUGUST 8, 1963: Fifteen thieves committed The Great Train Robbery in Britain and stole about $57 million today (£2.6 million). A £1 note from the heist sold for about $1,100 (£750) at J. P. Humbert Auctioneers in Northamptonshire, U.K., in 2015.

AUGUST 9, 1944: The debut of Smokey the Bear and his image and message have probably helped prevent many wildfires. A 1957 Smokey the Bear string holder sold for $152 on eBay in 2016. String holders are from the old days before paper and plastic bags when store purchases were wrapped in paper and tied with string. A string holder held the ball of string.

Smokey the Bear string holder
(Photo courtesy of eBay seller specks32499)

AUGUST 10, 1846: President James K. Polk signed an Act of Congress that established the Smithsonian Institution, America's collection. Today, it includes nineteen museums, the National Zoo, and nine research centers holding 138 million artifacts, works of art and specimens, and two million library volumes. It was established with a $500,000 bequest from the estate of James Smithson, an English scientist who never traveled to America. The Smithsonian preserves our greatest collection, from the Star-Spangled Banner flag that flew over Fort McHenry during the War of 1812 to the Apollo lunar landing module to one pair of Dorothy's ruby slippers from *The Wizard of Oz.*

The Star-Spangled Banner

AUGUST 10, 1932: The first Rin Tin Tin passed away, after almost fourteen human years. Rescued in WWI by Lee Duncan from a bombed French village, Rin Tin Tin captured the hearts of millions of kids and adults alike. His movies were hugely successful, and Warner Bros. paid him $2,000 per week (newyorker.com, 8/29/11).

The movie poster for his feature film, *Where the North Begins* (1923), a Style A one sheet, hunted down $2,070 in 2006 at Heritage Auctions.

Rin Tin Tin

(Photo courtesy of Heritage Auctions, HA. com)

AUGUST 11, 1919: Steel magnate and philanthropist Andrew Carnegie passed away after giving away hundreds of millions of dollars. He reportedly funded 3,000 libraries around the world.

A Tiffany Dragonfly table lamp from Andrew Carnegie's collection auctioned for $2,110,000 at Sotheby's in 2015.

Andrew Carnegie

The Tiffany Dragonfly lamp *(Photo courtesy of Sotheby's)*

AUGUST 12, 1881: Producer and director of more than eighty movies, Cecil B. DeMille debuted in life. In his blockbuster film, *The Ten Commandments*, Charlton Heston's own newborn son played the baby Moses, and in the burning bush scene, Heston was the voice of God. The movie required 14,000 extras and 15,000 animals (IMDb.com). Costing $13 million, it made $80 million worldwide (the-numbers.com).

In 2012, *The Ten Commandments* tablets from the movie, made of fiberglass and painted like red granite, sold for $36,250 at Julien's Live.

Cecil B. DeMille

AUGUST 13, 1860: The birthday of Phoebe Ann Mosey who became famous as Annie Oakley. A copy of the book *Annie Oakley of The Wild West* with her signature

Annie Oakley's Parker (*Photo courtesy of Heritage Auctions, HA.com*)

on an enclosed note and a penny she'd shot through the center, went for $3,000 on eBay in 2016 by Quinn's Auction. Her 16-gauge Parker Brothers hammer shotgun hit $293,000 at Heritage Auctions in 2013.

Annie Oakley

AUGUST 14, 1851: Birthday of O.K. Corral legend John Henry "Doc" Holliday. Doc's frock coat auctioned for $55,000, his pistol in a case for $50,000, and his dental chair for $40,000 at Guernsey's in 2013.

AUGUST 14, 2014: The highest price for a car sold in an auction was paid this day, $38 million for a 1962 Ferrari 250 GTO Berlinetta at Bonhams. The most ever paid for any car was in the private sale of a 1963 Ferrari 250 GTO racer for $52 million in 2013 (bloomberg. com, 10/2/13).

A 1962 Ferrari 250 GTO—not the $52 million Ferrari; this one is from the Ralph Lauren Collection, 2005

AUGUST 15, 1912: Chef and cookbook author Julia Child was born. A set of five copper pans owned by Julia Child from about the 1960s were valued at $3,500–$5,000 on PBS' *Antiques Roadshow* in 2013 (pbs.org).

AUGUST 15, 1935: Beloved cowboy humorist Will Rogers passed away this day in a small plane crash in Alaska, setting off national mourning.

A collection of photos of Rogers and his pilot Wiley Post prior to the crash—and of the plane upside down in the water after the crash—and some autographs, were appraised at $18,000 to $20,000 on the *Antiques Roadshow* in 2008 (pbs.org).

Will Rogers

Wiley Post

A few pearls from Will Rogers:

"Everything is funny, as long as it's happening to somebody else."

"Even if you're on the right track, you'll get run over if you just sit there."

"The only difference between death and taxes is that death doesn't get worse every time Congress meets" (All from brainyquote.com).

AUGUST 16, 1948: Babe Ruth succumbed to cancer this day, but his legend continues.

His c. 1920 New York Yankees game-worn jersey—his earliest known—reached $4.4 million at SCP Auctions in an Internet auction in 2012.

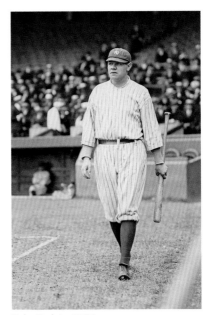

Babe Ruth's earliest known jersey (*Photo courtesy of SCP Auctions*)

Babe Ruth in 1920

AUGUST 16, 1854: Furniture and cabinetmaker Duncan Phyfe passed away this day. His furniture was in such demand in the late 18th and first half of the 19th centuries that he was known as the "United States Rage."

Duncan Phyfe

AUGUST 16, 1949: Margaret Mitchell, author of *Gone With The Wind*, passed away from injuries after being hit by a car. The driver, Hugh Gravitt, turned himself in and served almost eleven months in prison, two months on a chain gang (tulsaworld.com, 9/5/91). He died in 1994, still remorseful (orlandosentinel.com, 4/22/94).

(Continued on the next page.)

A 1938 edition of *Gone With the Wind* autographed by twenty-six cast members and two directors—including Clark Gable, Vivien Leigh, Olivia de Havilland, Leslie Howard, Hattie "Mammy" McDaniel, Butterfly "Prissy" McQueen, David O. Selznick, and Victor Fleming—ended at $135,300 at a Profiles in History auction in 2012.

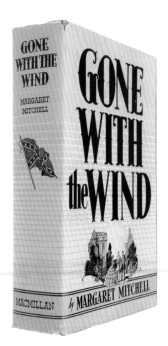

This first edition, first printing, May 1936 of *Gone with the Wind* inscribed by Margaret Mitchell with a signed note on her stationery sold for $17,925 at Heritage Auctions in 2008. *(Photo courtesy of Heritage Auctions)*

AUGUST 17, 1893: Playwright, screenwriter, and come-up-and-see-me-sometime actress Mae West made her entrance into the world. The surrealist artist Salvador Dali actually created a couch shaped like her lips in the 1930s, and one of the five made auctioned for £62,140 in 2003 at Christie's.

Mae West

AUGUST 18, 1992: Larry Bird announced his retirement from basketball. A member of the 1992 Olympic Basketball Dream Team, his USA game-worn jersey sold for $4,800 at Julien's in 2014. A game-used 1992 USA Olympic Dream Team basketball

Autographed Dream Team ball
(Courtesy of SCP Auctions)

went for $230,041 in 2015 at SCP Auctions. This multi-signed basketball (autographed by eleven players including Michael Jordan, Magic Johnson, and Larry Bird, plus Coach Daly) was used in their 117-85, gold medal-clinching victory over Croatia in Barcelona.

The Dream Team and the signed ball (*Courtesy of SCP Auctions*)

AUGUST 19: Philo T. Farnsworth, generally regarded as the inventor of the first working and patented television, was born in 1906. In 1921, Gene Roddenberry was born on this day and used TV to bring "Space, the final frontier" into our homes with *Star Trek*. Profiles in History sold Capt. Kirk's chair for $304,000 in 2002.

The original eleven-foot model of the Starship *Enterprise* is docked in the National Air and Space Museum in Washington, D.C. Principally designed by Matt Jefferies, it represented a ship 947 feet long and 417 feet wide (airandspace.si.edu/collections). Trekkies recognize the name *Jefferies* from "Jefferies tubes," which are tunnels for getting around inside the ship, and also the character "Captain Jefferies," one of the designers of the NX-class of starships (memory-alpha.wikia.com). Matt Jefferies also designed the phaser pistol and interior sets for the series, for which he received an Academy Award nomination for Art Direction and Scenic Design.

If this is too Trekkie for you, Jefferies was also art designer for: *The Old Man and the Sea* (1958), and for the TV shows *The Untouchables, Mission: Impossible, Little House on the Prairie*, and *Dallas*.

Philo T. Farnsworth

Marker in Riverside, Iowa, for the "Future Birthplace of James T. Kirk" (*Photo courtesy of Marshall Astor*)

(Continued on the next page.)

The original Starship *Enterprise* model (*Photo courtesy of FlugKerl2*)

The original phaser rifle used in only one episode by William Shatner went for $231,000 at Julien's Auctions in 2013. Created by toy designer Reuben Klamer, it was constructed of wood and had an aluminum barrel; blue-green metallic paint gave it that futuristic look (hollywoodreporter.com, 4/7/13).

Back to Earth, Groucho Marx, eighty-six, passed away this day in 1977.

AUGUST 20, 1667: Author John Milton's classic epic poem, *Paradise Lost*, was published. A first edition with a 1669 imprint auctioned for $16,250 at Bonhams in 2013.

AUGUST 21, 1911:
Italian Vincenzo Peruggia committed one of the greatest crimes in art history by stealing Leonardo da Vinci's *Mona Lisa* from the Louvre in Paris. He was arrested

Vincenzo Peruggia

The *Mona Lisa*

two years later in Italy, but he only served seven months of a one-year sentence. He was considered somewhat of a national hero for returning the famous painting to the homeland of Leonardo da Vinci . . . for a brief period of time.

AUGUST 22, 1880: Thanks to George Herriman's birth this day, Krazy Kat, was also born.

His original, hand-colored *Krazy Kat* Sunday comic from June 25, 1922, sold for $59,750 in 2013 at Heritage Auctions. Herriman drew twenty-four other comic strips during his career.

This day in 1920, Ray Bradbury was born; he wrote *Fahrenheit 451* and *The Martian Chronicles*.

George Herriman

AUGUST 23, 1926:

At the age of thirty-one, silent film star and national heartthrob Rudolph Valentino (Rodolfo Alfonso Raffaello Pierre Filibert Guglielmi

Valentino

di Valentina d'Antonguolla) died from infection after surgery for a perforated ulcer. His death reportedly caused chaos, riots, and fans to commit suicide. It is estimated 100,000 people paid their respects at his casket.

While his signed check and signed letter went for just $580 at Christie's in 2007, his 1926 estate auction catalog sold for $4,000 at Profiles in History in 2010.

The Son of Sheik poster (Photo courtesy of Heritage Auctions, HA.com)

It featured interior and exterior photos of his home in Beverly Hills, called Falcon Lair, and listed his stable of horses, purebred dogs, and cars for sale. In 2007, Valentino's *The Son of Sheik* movie poster sold for $4,182.50 at Heritage Auctions.

AUGUST 24, 79: Mount Vesuvius erupted, destroying Pompeii and Herculaneum and killing thousands. A *Last Days of Pompeii* (1913) one sheet movie poster made $2,151 in 2008 at Heritage Auctions. It was actually a remake of some earlier shorts (IMDb.com).

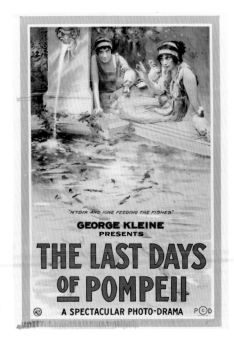

(*Photo courtesy of Heritage Auctions*)

AUGUST 25, 1930: The first James Bond was born, Sean Connery. Of the twenty-six Bond movies, Connery starred in seven; only Roger Moore acted in as many (classicfilm.about.com).

In 2015, Sir Sean sold two diamonds at Sotheby's: a pear-shaped 15.2-carat, pink diamond for $4,058,000 and a five-carat, pear-shaped diamond in a ring for $250,000.

Sean Connery
(*Photo: Dutch National Archives, The Hague, FotocollectieAlgemeenNederlandsPersbureau, ANeFo, 1945-1989*)

AUGUST 26, 1930: Lon Chaney, "The Man of a Thousand Faces," passed away. With more than 150 movie roles from 1913 to 1930 (IMDb.com) to his credit—including

Lon Chaney

Phantom of the Opera (1925) and *The Hunchback of Notre Dame* (1923)— it is fitting that the one sheet for his *London After Midnight* (1927) skyrocketed to $478,000 at Heritage Auctions in 2014, the most paid for a movie poster sold in a public auction. In it, he played a vampire. This was the only known copy of the one sheet version of this poster, making it the holy grail of movie poster collecting.

The truly rare *London After Midnight* (Photo courtesy of Heritage Auctions, HA.com)

AUGUST 27, 1576:

Titian

The Madonna and Child with Saints Luke and Catherine of Alexandria

Renaissance master Titian (Tiziano Vecelli) died in Venice of a fever while the city was being ravaged by the plague. Famous for painting *David and Goliath, The Rape of Europa, The Punishment of Tythus*, and many more, his *A Sacra Conversazione: The Madonna and Child with Saints Luke and Catherine of Alexandria* reached the height of $16,882,500 in 2011 at Sotheby's.

AUGUST 28, 2005: One of the four existing pairs of Dorothy's ruby slippers from *The Wizard of Oz* was stolen from the Judy Garland Museum in Grand Rapids, Minnesota (forbes.com, 12/3/08). When the thief or thieves broke in, security cameras and alarm systems were not working (minnesotamonthly.com, Feb. 2009). The slippers have not been recovered to date. A pair of ruby slippers could sell for millions of dollars.

Ruby slippers safe in the Smithsonian
(Photo courtesy of dbking)

AUGUST 29, 1877: The second President of The Church of Jesus-Christ of Latter-day Saints, Brigham Young passed away. In 2007, Swann Galleries sold an 1830 first edition Book of Mormon signed by Orson Pratt, an original member of the Quorum of Twelve Apostles, for $180,000. A second edition of the LDS Church hymnal went for the same price, $180,000 (deseretnews.com, 3/23/07).

Brigham Young

Orson Pratt in 1851

Left: The Book of Mormon *(Photo courtesy of Swann Auction Galleries)* Right: Page inscribed by Orson Pratt *(Photo courtesy of Swann Auction Galleries)*

AUGUST 29, 1958: Michael Jackson popped into the world. In 2015, the Record Industry Association of America reported that *Thriller* had sold 100 million albums worldwide, and Michael Jackson had 1 billion sales overall. More than 13 million of his albums have sold since his death on June 25, 2009 (yahoo.com, 6/26/17).

Jackson's sequined white glove went with a flourish for $350,000 at Julien's in 2009.

Michael Jackson, 1988 *(Photo courtesy of Zoran Veselinovic)*

AUGUST 29, 1982: The Swedish movie star Ingrid Bergman passed away this day, sixty-seven years to the day after she was born in 1915. It was her character "Illsa," not "Rick," in *Casablanca* that uttered that iconic line, "Play it again, Sam," referring to the song, "As Time Goes By."

Ingrid Bergman

This *Casablanca* window card sold for $5,975 at Heritage Auctions in 2012. *(Photo courtesy of Heritage Auctions)*

[Continued on the next page.]

The piano that Sam (Dooley Wilson) played at her request in Rick's Café sold for $3.4 million at Bonhams in 2014. Another piano seen briefly in the movie tuned up $602,500 at Sotheby's in December 2012.

AUGUST 29, 1966: The last public performance of the Beatles. The Fab Four played in Candlestick Park in San Francisco to about 24,000 people, not filling the venue.

In 2011, John Lennon's decayed and extracted molar sold for £23,000 at Omega Auctions in the U.K.

The Beatles

AUGUST 30, 1797: The birthday of Mary Wollstonecraft Shelley, the "mother" of *Frankenstein*. She was married to the poet Percy Bysshe Shelley. Published in 1818, *Frankenstein* was a horror classic in print and on film.

It was reported in 2013 that Lord Byron's first edition of the book was sold in 2012 by Peter Harrington, London, a rare books dealer. It was inscribed by Mary Shelley, "To Lord Byron, from the author." Lord Byron was a friend

Mary Shelley

of the family. The sales price was not reported, but the asking price was: £350,000 (telegraph.co.uk, 1/18/13). Also, a three sheet Style C movie poster from 1931 sold for $358,500 at Heritage Auctions in 2015.

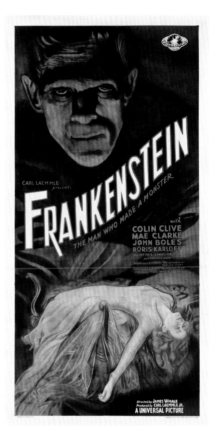

(Photo courtesy of Heritage Auctions, HA.com)

AUGUST 31, 1897: Thomas A. Edison received a patent for his Kinetoscope, which was not the first moving pictures projector. The zoopraxiscope was invented by Englishman Eadweard Muybridge in 1879, and it used spinning disks of glass to project images, simulating motion. Muybridge was the early photographer who executed the famous experiment with a series of synchronized cameras to prove that all four of a horse's hooves leave the ground at one point while galloping. Credit must also be given to William Kennedy Laurie Dickson who worked for Edison and actually developed the Kinetoscope.

A zoopraxiscope disc

An illustration of a Kinetoscope showing the interior and the peephole on the top

SEPTEMBER

SEPTEMBER 1: Edgar Rice Burroughs, 1875; Yvonne de Carlo, 1922; and undefeated Heavyweight Champion Rocky Marciano, 1923, celebrated birthdays. Burroughs wrote dozens of novels about Tarzan and about adventurers on the Moon, Mars, and Venus and also *The Land That Time Forgot*. A shout-out for the first appearance of *Tarzan of the Apes* in *The All-Story Magazine*, October 1912. Even though heavily worn and stained, a copy of it brought $21,250 at Heritage Auctions in 2015.

Yvonne De Carlo

Yvonne De Carlo's black cape with red lining from *The Munsters* sold for $3,125 in 2014 at Bonhams. Rocky Marciano's fight-worn boxing gloves and a signed photo from the 1950s hit $8,400 at Sotheby's in 2005.

SEPTEMBER 2, 1973: J.R.R. Tolkien passed away, but his tales live on. Though he did not live to see it, all of *The Hobbit* and *The Lord of the Rings* movies have raked in $5.89 billion to date with production costs of about $1 billion (the-numbers. com).

J.R.R. Tolkien

A presentation copy of *The Hobbit* inscribed and signed by Tolkien commanded £137,000 at Sotheby's in 2015. Gollum's "Precious," "The One Ring," the penultimate production prototype ring of gold, slipped away for $12,800 at Julien's Auctions in 2013. Other prototypes of the ring were made in gold and silver. John "Gimli" Rhys-Davies' double-headed battle-axe sold for $185,000 at the same auction.

SEPTEMBER 3, 1944: H. Ty Warner was born, and sometime in 1993, so was the Beanie Baby. Warner made billions of dollars with the toy that was feverishly collected . . . and then wasn't . . . and now some are. The purple Princess Diana Beanie is offered for stratospheric prices while other so-called rare Beanies sell for

(Continued on the next page.)

several hundred dollars. A magenta Canadian embroidered #4052 New Face Teddy Bear with 1994 tag sold for $812 on eBay in 2016. (Other similar Beanies have sold for less.)

A Beanie, "Sizzle the Bear" (*Photo courtesy of Jonny, CC BY-SA 3.0*)

SEPTEMBER 4: In 1886, Geronimo surrendered and was a prisoner for the rest of his life. Even so, he was invited to be a part of the 1904 St. Louis World's Fair.

An 1886 Winchester owned by Army Captain Henry W. Lawton, who led the cavalry troopers in the capture of Geronimo, sold for $1,265,000 at Rock Island Auction in 2016. It was the highest paid to date for a firearm at auction.

Henry Lawton

Geronimo

SEPTEMBER 4, 1893: Beatrix Potter told the story of Peter Rabbit for the first time in a letter she illustrated. *The Tale of Peter Rabbit* was turned down by several publishers, so Beatrix Potter published it herself in 1901. One of the initial 250 printed, a first edition, first issue with a brown cover, sold for $75,000 in 2014 at Sotheby's.

Beatrix Potter

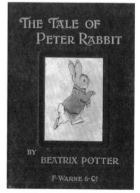

A 1902 first edition of *The Tale of Peter Rabbit* published by Frederick Warne & Co.

In 1950, Mort Walker's GI goof-off *Beetle Bailey* began life in syndication, where he still gets into trouble today.

SEPTEMBER 5: The first fuel pump was sold in 1885. Since this was before the first appearance of cars, it dispensed kerosene.

In 2016, Mecum Auctions sold a Refiners gasoline pump globe for $55,000.

Refiner's gas globe
(Photo courtesy of Mecum.com)

SEPTEMBER 6, 1622: The Spanish galleons *Nuestra Senora de Atocha* and the *Santa Margarita* sank in a hurricane near Key West, Florida. On July 20, 1985, the $450 million Atocha Mother Lode treasure was found by Mel Fisher—40+ tons of silver in addition to gold and emeralds (melfisher.com). A gold and emerald cross from the *Atocha* was blessed with $118,750 at Guernsey's in 2015.

The *Atocha* cross *(Photo courtesy of Guernsey's)*

SEPTEMBER 7, 1813: *The Troy Post* newspaper in New York was the first to record the United States being referred to as "Uncle Sam."

A 1917 J.M. Flagg *Uncle Sam* poster sold for $20,000 at Guernsey's in 2015.

SEPTEMBER 7, 1860: Anna Mary Robertson Moses was born. She began painting at the age of seventy-eight and became the famous folk artist Grandma Moses.

In 2006, her 1943 *Sugaring Off*, a snowy landscape of making maple syrup, sold for $1.36 million. A smaller version of *Sugaring Off* went for $254,500 in 2010, both at Christie's.

Grandma Moses

SEPTEMBER 8: In 1998, Mark McGwire hit home run #70 to break the record for the most home runs in a season. That ball went over the fence at Guernsey's for $3 million in 1999. McGwire's record was broken in 2001 by Barry Bonds who hit seventy-three.

In 1504, Michelangelo hit an artistic grand slam when he unveiled his priceless, seventeen-foot-tall marble masterpiece, *David*.

David (Photo courtesy of Jörg Bittner Unna)

SEPTEMBER 9, 1606: VOC

Enkhuizen, a Dutch company, sold stock to Pieter Hermanszoon boode, and his stock share certificate—the oldest known to date—was found by student Ruben Schalk at the Utrecht University in the Netherlands in 2010.

The oldest stock certificate—the second page shows dividend payments

SEPTEMBER 10, 1929: Arnold Palmer was born and became a great force in the world of golf. He went on to win four Masters and two British Opens.

In 2012, $41,825 was the winning bid at Heritage Auctions for Arnold Palmer's first set of golf clubs and bag from the 1940s.

Arnold Palmer

SEPTEMBER 11, 1297: William Wallace's men defeated an English army at Stirling Bridge, Scotland.

In 2001, Mel Gibson's fifty-two-inch sword used in *Braveheart* brought down $170,000 for charity (for fighting mother-to-child AIDS transmission in Zambia) at Sotheby's.

The William Wallace statue in Aberdeen, Scotland

SEPTEMBER 12, 1857: The wooden side-wheeler steamship SS *Central America* sank in a hurricane off North Carolina, taking more than 400 people to the bottom—along with tons of gold (estimates range from three to twenty tons). The largest ingot retrieved from the ocean floor weighed eighty pounds; it was called "Eureka" for its size and because it came from the California gold fields. Eureka sold for $8 million in 2001 to a private buyer (sfgate.com, 11/9/01).

SEPTEMBER 13, 1911: Bill Monroe was born to be the Father of Bluegrass. His career as a musician spanned sixty-nine years.

In 2009, his heavily worn, seven-inch mandolin tuned up $37,500 at Christie's.

SEPTEMBER 14, 1914: The Lone Ranger Clayton Moore was born. While most remember him for his 169 episodes in the TV series, he also acted in more than forty movies (IMDb.com).

In 2014, his outfit (gun belt, Colts, blue shirt, pants, Stetson hat, boots, and red kerchief) said, "Hi-Yo, Silver! Away!" and rode off for $195,000 from A&S Auction Co. in Waco, Texas. One of his masks, his gloves, and Tonto's headband sold for $12,000 at Profiles in History in 2010.

The Lone Ranger and Silver

SEPTEMBER 14, 1975:
An unemployed and unbalanced teacher slashed Rembrandt's *The Night Watch*. It had been previously cut in 1911 and had acid sprayed on it in 1990. It was restored each time, but the abuse slightly shows.

The Night Watch

SEPTEMBER 15: Birthdays include James Fenimore Cooper, 1789; Agatha Christie, 1890; and Fay Wray, 1907. Cooper's *The Last of the Mohicans: A Narrative of 1757*, published in 1826, sold at Skinners for $492 in 2015.

James Fenimore Cooper

(Photo courtesy of Heritage Auctions, HA.com)

161

(Continued on the next page.)

In 2014, a trunk containing a locked strongbox purchased at an estate sale in author Agatha Christie's home yielded heirlooms that reached nearly £50,000 at auction at Bonhams in London. Inside was found a diamond ring, gold coins, and a diamond brooch. The owner didn't get around to forcing the strongbox open until four years after the sale (telegraph.co.uk, 10/9/14).

In 1999, an original 1933 *King Kong* poster, 41 x 81 inches and with Fay Wray, was a hit at $244,500 at Sotheby's. There were many versions of this blockbuster's poster. A 1933 Style B three sheet, 40.25 x 79 inches, went for the gargantuan price of $388,375 at Heritage Auctions in 2012.

Fay Wray

SEPTEMBER 16, 1925: The great blues guitarist and singer B.B. King was born. At a gig early in his career, a fight over a woman called Lucille turned over a container of kerosene that started a fire. King ran out of the building and then back in to save his guitar. From then on, he named all his guitars "Lucille" to remember to never do that again (npr.org, 5/15/15).

A B.B. King-signed, black Epiphone, hollow-body electric guitar, a reissue of Gibson's ES-335, hit $1,792.50 at Heritage Auctions in 2009.

The signed guitar

Riley B. "B.B." King

SEPTEMBER 16, 1956: David Copperfield magically appeared. His International Museum and Library of Conjuring Arts contains 80,000 pieces, including books dating to the 16th century and much of Harry Houdini's memorabilia (davidcopperfield.com).

Copperfield owned the Best Director Oscar for *Casablanca* for a time, buying it in 2003 for $232,000. He sold it in 2012 for $2+ million (deadline.com, 4/3/13).

David Copperfield (*Photo courtesy of Homer Liwag*)

SEPTEMBER 17, 1796: President George Washington's Farewell Address, saying he would not seek a third term, was published in a newspaper (US Dept. of State, Office of Historian). It was not given in a speech.

A nineteen-page pamphlet imprint titled, "President Washington's Resignation, and Address To The Citizens of the United States, September 17, 1796," auctioned for $3,500 at Heritage Auctions in 2014. Also that year, Keno Auctions brokered the sale of Washington's first presidential Thanksgiving Proclamation, 1789, to a private buyer. It was offered for $8.4 million.

George Washington, 1772

SEPTEMBER 18, 1905: Greta Garbo was born in Sweden. She was a star of silent movies and talkies with 30+ movie credits during the 1920s and '30s (IMdb.com).

Some of the highlights of Julien's 2012 auction of her estate items included: a Louis Vuitton steamer trunk, $37,500; a "GG" monogrammed sterling cocktail set, $34,375; and a gold Verdura compact, $35,200.

Greta Garbo

SEPTEMBER 19, 1911: Englishman William Golding, author of *Lord of the Flies*, was born. He was awarded the Nobel Prize for literature in 1983 and knighted in 1988.

A first edition signed by Golding with dust jacket sold for $11,121 at Sotheby's in 2002. Without the signature and dust jacket, the price drops like a rock.

William
Golding

SEPTEMBER 20, 1934: Don Quixote's Dulcinea was born in Rome. Sophia Loren has more than ninety film credits, and she has won four Golden Globes and an Academy Award (for *Two Women*, not *Man of La Mancha*).

A purple Georgio Armani purse she once owned sold for $287,000 in a 2011 charity auction to help Siberian children (yahoo.com/news, 11/30/11).

Sophia Loren
(Photo courtesy of Allan Warren)

SEPTEMBER 21, 1832: The book closed today on *Ivanhoe* author Sir Walter Scott of Scotland. In 2014, his mahogany writing desk and its contents (twenty-eight returned checks and a letter) auctioned at Lyons & Turnbull for $8,515.

Sir Walter Scott

SEPTEMBER 21, 1866: Author H.G. Wells was born to amaze with sci-fi classics like *The Time Machine, The War of the Worlds,* and *The Invisible Man.*

In 2013, Swann Galleries brought in $24,600 for a first edition of *The First Men in the Moon* (1901).

H.G. Wells

SEPTEMBER 22, 1776: The hanging of Captain Nathan Hale by British troops for being a spy. His true-patriot last words were: "I only regret that I have but one life to lose for my country."

Hale's signature auctioned for $8,050 in 1997 at Christie's.

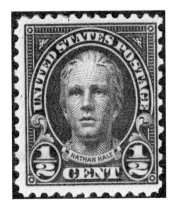

1925 Nathan Hale stamp

SEPTEMBER 22, 2015: The all-around great guy Yogi Berra passed away. In 2016, his 1950s New York Yankees, game-used and autographed catcher's mask made $29,586 at Grey Flannel Auctions. In 2013, his 1955 American League MVP plaque hit $36,098.50 at Goldin Auctions. Yogi's 1948 Bowman #6 Mint 9 rookie card went for $20,315 in 2016 at Heritage Auctions.

Yogi was famous for his sayings, and everyone has heard, "It's déjà vu all over again." But have you heard these Yogi-isms?

"Half the lies they tell about me aren't true."

"A nickel ain't worth a dime anymore."

"Baseball is ninety percent mental. The other half is physical."

Yogi's rookie card (*Photo courtesy of Heritage Auctions, HA.com*)

"The future ain't what it used to be." (bustle.com, 9/23/15)

SEPTEMBER 23, 1930: Raymond Charles Robinson was one of the greatest soul singers and songwriters ever born. He won several Grammy Awards and was inducted into several halls of fame. He passed away on June 10, 2004.

Julien's Live sold Ray Charles' keyboard for $3,840.

Ray Charles (*Photo courtesy of Rob Bogaerts, ANEFO*)

SEPTEMBER 24: Born today were author F. Scott Fitzgerald, 1896, and Muppet maker Jim Henson, 1936. Theodor "Dr. Seuss" Geisel passed away in 1991.

A first edition of *The Great Gatsby* by Fitzgerald, 1925, with the rare, original blue dustjacket with the graphic of a disembodied woman's face brought $377,000 at Sotheby's in 2014. A Fizzgig puppet from Henson's *The Dark Crystal* sold at the Prop Store in 2015 for £22,500. In 2015, Dr. Seuss' *How The Grinch Stole Christmas,* a sixteen-field production cel setup of the Whos in Whoville singing "Welcome, Christmas" while encircling a decorated Christmas tree, sold for $6,752.50 at Heritage Auctions. It was animated by the legendary cartoonist and three-time Academy Award winner Chuck Jones, who was born on Sept. 21, 1912.

The Whos singing in Whoville (*Photo courtesy of Heritage Auctions, HA.com*)

F. Scott Fitzgerald

Dr. Seuss

Jim Henson with George Lucas

SEPTEMBER 25, 1951:

There was a stirring in the Force this day when Mark Hamill was born.

The movie-used model of Luke Skywalker's X-Wing Fighter sold in 2012 for $221,400 at Profiles in History.

The model of Luke's X-Wing Fighter (*Photos courtesy of Profiles in History*)

SEPTEMBER 25, 1903: Artist Mark Rothko arrived to bring new meaning to emotions on canvas, expressed as bands of color. His *Orange, Red, Yellow* splashed at Christie's for $86,882,500 in 2012.

Mark Rothko

SEPTEMBER 26: Appearing this day were George Gershwin, 1898; *The Beverly Hillbillies* TV show, 1962; and *The Brady Bunch*, 1969. The composer of "The Rhapsody in Blue," Gershwin also composed "Second Rhapsody," c. 1931; an autographed manuscript of it with thirteen bars of music and inscribed with, "From sketch book of 2nd Rhapsody, George Gershwin," fetched $46,875 in 2014 at Heritage Auctions.

George Gershwin

The dilapidated-looking *Beverly Hillbillies* truck roared to $275,000 at Barrett-Jackson in 2015. It was one of five created by George Barris. Everything Jed touches turns to money.

While *The Brady Bunch* won no Emmy during its five seasons, it did win the TV Land Awards for: Favorite Made-for-TV Maid, Ann B. Davis; Favorite TV Food, "Pork Chops and Applesauce"; and a Pop Culture Award.

SEPTEMBER 27, 1956: Super athlete Mildred E. "Babe" Didrikson Zaharias passed away. She had forty-one LPGA tour wins, and she won two gold medals in track and field at the 1932 Olympics. Baseball, softball, basketball, diving, bowling—she did it all.

Her golf bag and fourteen clubs hit $31,250 at Nate D. Sanders auction in 2014. A 1940s signed photo of Babe Didrikson Zaharias went for $1,553.50 at Heritage Auctions in 2012.

"Babe" Didrikson Zaharias

SEPTEMBER 28, 1066: William the Conqueror invaded England and became king. In 2014, a William I the Conqueror penny, c. 1083-86, sold for $1,292.50 at Heritage Auctions.

William the Conqueror penny (*Photo courtesy of Heritage Auctions, HA.com*)

William the Conqueror depicted on a tapestry

SEPTEMBER 28, 1987: *Star Trek: The Next Generation* premiered, and in 2006, a replica of the Starship *Enterprise-D* from the show conquered $576,000 at Christie's.

Patrick (Jean-Luc Picard) Stewart at the premier of *The Martian*

SEPTEMBER 29, 1547: Coincidentally, Miguel de Cervantes Saavedra was born in the same month as Sophia Loren. His novel, *The Ingenious Hidalgo Don Quixote de la Mancha*, has been hailed as among the best in Spanish literature, and 500+ million copies of it have sold.

A third authorized edition from 1605 (authorized because there were knock-offs in those days, too) sold for $116,500 in 2012 at Christie's.

Don Quixote

Earlier in life, Cervantes was captured by pirates at the beginning of his military career and kept in prison for about five years until ransomed.

The windmill scene from
Don Quixote (*Gustave
Doré, illustrator*)

SEPTEMBER 29, 1935: The Killer was born. Jerry Lee Lewis had many hits, including "Great Balls of Fire," "Whole Lotta Shakin' Going On," and the Big Bopper's "Chantilly Lace."

In 2015, his 1959 Harley-Davidson FLH Duo-Glide sold for $385,000 at Mecum Auctions (money.cnn.com, 1/24/15).

The Killer's 1959 Harley-Davidson FLH Duo-Glide (*Photo
courtesy Mecum Auctions*)

Jerry Lee Lewis

SEPTEMBER 30: Truman Capote, the author of two novels that are the exact opposite of each other, *Breakfast at Tiffany's* and *In Cold Blood*, was born in 1924.

At an auction of his estate in 2006 at Bonhams, a diamond, emerald, gold, and platinum ring took down $16,730, and a 1965 first edition, autographed *In Cold Blood* sold for $8,365.

Truman Capote

SEPTEMBER 30, 1955: Rising star James Dean did not survive a car accident. In his short five-year film career, he acted in thirty-one movies, won two Golden Globes and received two Academy Award nominations, posthumously (IMDb.com).

A white t-shirt James Dean wore in *Rebel Without a Cause* sold for $11,352.50 at Heritage Auctions in 2006.

James Dean

SEPTEMBER 30, 2015:

George Reeves' Superman costume from the TV show's second season (the last one in black and white) sold for $216,000 at Profiles in History. The sale also included the "flying pan" apparatus that he laid on so special effects could make him fly. In 2008, a *Superman and the Mole Men* (1951) movie poster featuring George Reeves went for $4,182.50 at Heritage Auctions.

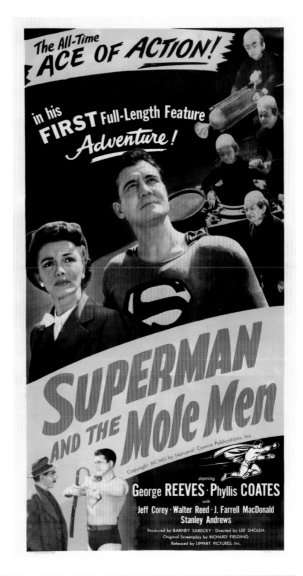

George Reeves in *Superman and the Mole Men* (*Photo courtesy of Heritage Auctions, HA.com*)

OCTOBER

OCTOBER 1, 1880: Composer of "The Stars and Stripes Forever" John Philip Sousa assumed command of the United States Marine Band on this day.

A framed photo of him with a 1901 autographed musical notation sold for $235 at Cowan's in 2014.

John Philip Sousa

OCTOBER 1, 1908: Henry Ford introduced the Model T. In 2015, Barrett-Jackson sold a restored Tin Lizzy painted red with serial number 90 (of 15 million made) for $121,000.

OCTOBER 1, 1935: Birthday of Julie Andrews. Her many films include favorites *Mary Poppins* and *The Sound of Music*. She has won one Academy Award (*Mary Poppins*, 1964), five Golden Globes, and two Primetime Emmy Awards. She voiced the Queen in *Shrek 2* and *3* and Gru's mother in *Despicable Me* (IMDb.com).

Julie Andrews' Maria costumes worn in *The Sound of Music* hit a high note of $1.3 million in 2013, and Mary Poppins' "bottomless carpetbag" went to a new home for $95,000 in 2010, both at Profiles in History.

Julie Andrews

OCTOBER 2, 1890: The great comedian "Groucho" Julius Henry Marx was born this day and tickled funny bones with his TV show *You Bet Your Life* and movies like *Duck Soup* and *A Day at the Races* (Imdb. com).

Five items from the Marx Brothers, including a cigar and a photo signed by Groucho, a photo and postcard signed by Chico, and a contract signed by Harpo and Zeppo, fetched $1,276 at Robert Edward Auctions in 2006.

Groucho Marx

OCTOBER 3, 1226: St. Francis of Assisi passed away today. He is credited with recreating the Nativity with live animals and people; this grew into non-live manger scenes, or crèches.

Neapolitan crèche figures from the eighteenth and nineteenth centuries with realistic features and clothing are sought. In 2016, Skinner Auctioneers sold a Neapolitan crèche terracotta and wooden angel figure from the late eighteenth century for $2,460.

The Stigmata of St. Francis, c. 1487

OCTOBER 3: An important day in TV history with the premiers of: *The Mickey Mouse Club* that aired for fourteen seasons intermittently from 1955 to 1996; *Captain Kangaroo* that ran for almost thirty years from 1955 to 1984; *The Real McCoys* with Walter Brennan in 1957; *The Andy Griffith Show* in 1960; and *The Dick Van*

Dyke Show in 1961, which won fifteen Primetime Emmy Awards and two Golden Globes during just five seasons (IMDb.com).

In 2013, Mr. Moose and Bunny Rabbit—obtained from Bob Keeshan, Captain Kangaroo himself—sold at Nate D. Sanders Auction for $224,579. The only other set of these puppets is in the Smithsonian.

Dancing Bear, the Captain, Mr. Green Jeans, Bunny Rabbit, and Mr. Moose

Mr. Moose and Bunny Rabbit (*Photo courtesy of Nate D. Sanders Auctions*)

Cast of *The Dick Van Dyke Show*

The Mouseketeers in 1957; Annette Funicello is bottom left

OCTOBER 4, 1923: The birthday of Charlton Heston (birth name Charlton John Carter). He is not too well known for his stint on *The Bold and The Beautiful* soap opera in 1993 but is famous for *The Ten Commandments, Ben-Hur, Planet of the Apes, The Agony and The Ecstasy, Soylent Green,* and many others (IMDb.com).

Memorabilia from his estate was auctioned in March 2016 by Bonhams, and his personal script for *Ben-Hur* sold for $12,500.

Charlton Heston

OCTOBER 4, 1861: Frederic Remington, the sculptor and artist, was born—not to be confused with gunsmith Eliphat Remington who was born on October 28, 1793 and died on August 12, 1861, not long before Frederic's birth.

A master in depicting the Old West in bronze and paint, Frederic Remington's bronze sculpture, *The Wounded Bunkie* (of a trooper supporting his wounded comrade in the saddle, both at full gallop), brought the highest price for a Remington at $5,641,000 at Sotheby's in 2008.

Frederic Remington featured on a 1940s 10¢ stamp

Remington's *The Wounded Bunkie* (*Photo courtesy of Sotheby's*)

OCTOBER 4, 1895: The birth of Joseph F. "Buster" Keaton, a silent movie comic actor and stunt daredevil. Called "The Great Stone Face" because no situation seemed to faze him, Keaton performed his own stunts and was a master at falling down, even from heights. His most famous stunt was of an actual wall of a huge house falling on him in *Steamboat Bill, Jr.* (1928). Keaton was unscathed due to an open window in the wall that fell around him. This scene was shot in one take—there were no practice shots to make sure he would be safe. Watch it on You Tube. An original script from

Steamboat Bill Jr. pressbook (*Photo courtesy of Heritage Auctions, HA.com*)

his great train movie, *The General*, sold for $4,160 at Julien's Live in 2014. A pressbook with multiple pages from *Steamboat Bill, Jr.* auctioned for $1,553.50 in 2013; in 2008, one sold for $5,975, both at Heritage Auctions.

Buster Keaton in *Out West*, 1918

Buster Keaton

OCTOBER 5, 1902: Birthday of Louis Feinberg, aka Larry Fine, of slapstick masters The Three Stooges. Moe and Larry were the base of the troupe, and Moe's

(*Bottom*) Larry Fine, Moe Howard, and (*top*) Curly Howard

Moe's check to Larry (*Photo courtesy of Heritage Auctions*)

brothers Shemp and Curly alternated in the third spot over the years, eventually replaced by other actors. Larry had 234 screen credits during the years of 1930-1970, and the Stooges have a star on the Hollywood Walk of Fame (IMDb.com).

A check signed by Moe to Larry for $112.22 dated May 15, 1961 and endorsed by Larry on the back, framed with their photos, sold for $1,792.50 at Heritage Auctions in 2010.

OCTOBER 6, 2006:

A c. 1900 copper Indian Chief weathervane pointed to $5,840,000 at Sotheby's for bidders Jerry and Susan Lauren (Jerry is the brother of designer Ralph Lauren). The weathervane was from the J.L. Mott Iron Works and was previously owned by the granddaughter of Henry Ford. To date, this is the most ever paid for a weathervane.

The $5.84 million weathervane
(*Photo, courtesy of Sotheby's*)

OCTOBER 7, 1856:

Moses Fleetwood "Fleet" Walker was born and is considered by many to be the first African American in Major League Baseball, playing one season for the Toledo Blue Stockings in 1884. His brother also played for the team later in the season. Fleet attended the University of Michigan and played for the team there. In 1889, the Major Leagues erected the color barrier.

Also in sports news, on this day in 1916, Georgia Tech's football team defeated Cumberland College of Lebanon, Tennessee, 222-0.

Michigan Varsity Baseball Team, '82
Rollins, 3b and cf   Davis, rf   Autie, p and cf
Harvey, Captain and ss   Allmendinger, lf   Packard, p and 3b   Walker, c   Davenport, 1b   Dott, 2b

The University of Michigan's baseball team; Fleet is seated, third from the right. This cabinet card sold for $6,380 in 2006 at Robert Edward Auctions. (*Photo courtesy Robert Edward Auctions*)

"Fleet" Walker

OCTOBER 7, 1849: The passing of Edgar Allan Poe. Known for writing *The Raven, Murders in the Rue Morgue, The Tell-Tale Heart, The Pit and the Pendulum,* and other macabre stories, his first (and self) published work is probably his rarest. Poe wrote the forty-page *Ta-*

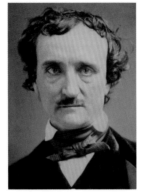

Edgar Allan Poe

Tamerlane

merlane and Other Poems, but did not name himself as the author. Listing only that it was written "By A Bostonian," it was not his finest work, and only about fifty copies were published. About a dozen still exist. Consequently, it is somewhat of a literary holy grail. In 2009, a copy sold at Christie's for $662,500.

OCTOBER 8, 1871: The Great Chicago Fire ignited and burned for two days, destroying about three square miles and killing 300 people. It started in the area of the O'Leary's barn, but the exact cause was never determined.

Photos of the ruins sell for a few dollars. An original panoramic photo, 32 x 9.5 inches and titled, *Chicago, as Seen after the Great Conflagration,* by Joshua Smith, sold for $262.90 at Heritage Auctions in 2012.

Chicago in Flames by Currier and Ives, 1871

OCTOBER 8, 1890: The birth of World War I Ace Eddie Rickenbacker who downed twenty-two planes and four defended observation balloons (nytimes.com, 7/24/73); he received the Medal of Honor. Rickenbacker also competed in the Indianapolis 500 four times before the war, and he bought the Indianapolis Motor Speedway afterwards.

Rickenbacker survived two plane crashes, the second a ditching in the Pacific. He and the plane's crew were adrift at sea for twenty-four days in 1942. They survived in part due to a seagull landing on Rickenbacker's head.

A signed copy of *Rickenbacker an Autobiography*, 1967, earned $216 in 2012.

Eddie Rickenbacker, c. 1918 (*Photo courtesy of Auburn University Libraries Special Collections and Archives*)

OCTOBER 9, 1888:

The Washington Monument opened to the public. Designed by Robert Mills who initially planned an obelisk on top of a structure of columns, the Monument is the tallest all-stone structure and tallest obelisk in the world at 554 feet, 7.3 inches.

Robert Mills' proposed design

The Washington Monument under construction, c. 1860, by Matthew Brady

Construction began in 1848 but halted in 1854 when funds ran out. The Civil War and disagreements about the design held up construction until 1877. The total cost was about $2.6 million.

In 1908, a baseball was dropped from the top of the Washington Monument thirteen times before Gabby Street, catcher for the Washington Senators, could glove it. He said in a newspaper article: "The ball I caught hit my mitt with terrific force, much greater than any pitched ball I have ever caught. . . . Though my mitt

[Continued on the next page.]

is three or four inches thick, the force of the ball benumbed my hand." The ball hit his catcher's glove with the sound of a rifle shot and 200 pounds of force (Heritage Auctions, 2008 October Signature Sports Collectibles Auction #710).

OCTOBER 10, 1924: Edward D. Wood, Jr., was born, but not to be a successful movie director. His infamous *Plan 9 from Outer Space* has been called the worst movie of all time. However, other movies are contenders for that title, and it is doubtful their movie posters bring thousands of dollars as *Plan 9* one sheets do—a very fine copy in 2008 brought $5,078.75 at Heritage Auctions.

Plan 9 from Outer Space (Photo courtesy of Heritage Auctions)

OCTOBER 10, 1985: Orson Welles passed away. He directed, starred in, and co-wrote *Citizen Kane* (1941), for which he won an Oscar for Original Screenplay. In 2011, that Oscar rose to $861,542 at Nate D. Sanders Auctions.

Orson Welles

Orson Welles' Oscar (*Photo courtesy of Nate D. Sanders Auctions*)

OCTOBER 11, 2011: Actor Richard Gere's 107-lot collection of guitars hit a high note of $936,438 at Christie's. At the top was a 1960 Gibson Les Paul that realized $98,500.

Richard Gere (*Photo courtesy of Neil Grabowsky/Montclair Film Festival*)

OCTOBER 11, 1965: American photographer Dorothy Lange passed away. Known worldwide for her photos of the Depression Era, her photo *Migrant Mother* made $134,500 in 2011 at Christie's.

Migrant Mother

Dorothy Lange

OCTOBER 12, 1492: Christopher Columbus landed in the Bahamas.

In 2015, a letter he wrote from Spain to his son Diego dated April 29, 1498 and valued at £15 million, was barred by a judge from leaving Spain to be auctioned (theguardian.co.uk, 3/11/2015).

Christopher Columbus

OCTOBER 12, 1989: A sad day for Rocky and Bullwinkle, cartoonist Jay Ward passed away. In addition to the flying squirrel and the often-befuddle moose from Frostbite Falls, Minnesota, Ward produced George of the Jungle, Dudley Do-Right, Peabody and Sherman, Super Chicken, Tom Slick, and other cartoons. Beloved by kids—and secretly by some adults who caught the puns—here are a few Bullwinkle-isms:

Bullwinkle: "Well, if you can't believe what you read in a comic book, what can you believe?"

Bullwinkle: "Well this is a pickle . . . actually it's more of a kumquat."

Rocky: "Do you know what an A-bomb is?"

Bullwinkle: "Certainly. A bomb is what some people call our show" (bullwinkle.toonzone.net).

Memorabilia from *The Bullwinkle Show* at Heritage Auctions really raked it in at $131.45 in 2013. The collection included an Exceptional Adequacy Award ribbon, "For helping to promote public apathy toward the Bullwinkle Show." The ribbon was given at a party celebrating the show being picked up by NBC.

The Exceptional Adequacy Award (*Photo courtesy of Heritage Auctions, HA.com*)

OCTOBER 13, 1860: James Wallace Black took the first aerial photograph in America of Boston from a hot air balloon piloted by Samuel Archer King. Titled, *Boston, as the Eagle and the Wild Goose See It*, the photo was taken from 1,200 feet. It is in the collection of the Metropolitan Museum of Art.

Boston, as the Eagle and the Wild Goose See It

OCTOBER 14, 1926: *Winnie-the-Pooh* was published by A.A. Milne about a boy named Christopher Robin, just like his own son. Pooh, Tigger, Eeyore, and Rabbit have been wildly successful in books, on TV, on radio, in movies, and in the theater.

In 2014, a drawing by E.H. Shepard in the second book, *The House At Pooh Corner*, of Christopher Robin looking over a fence and Pooh looking through it and titled, "For a long time they looked at the river beneath them," auctioned for $492,727 at Sotheby's.

E.H. Shepard's drawing (*Photo courtesy of Sotheby's*)

OCTOBER 15, 1920: Oh, Godfather, Mario Puzo was born. In addition to writing several novels, he was also the screenwriter or co-writer of the three Godfather movies, three Superman movies, *Earthquake*, and several other movies.

His forty-five-box archive sold for $625,000 at RR Auction in 2016. It included his 1965 Olympia typewriter, a 744-page draft for a book titled *Mafia*, which would later be renamed *The Godfather*, and two of his handwritten notes saying, "I'll make him an offer he can't refuse."

OCTOBER 16, 1758: The birth of Noah Webster who brought order to communication by publishing in 1828 the *American Dictionary of the English Language*, otherwise known as *Webster's Dictionary*. What would he think of the language today?

Two leaves from the original manuscript in the handwriting of Noah Webster excelled at $17,500 at Doyle's New York in 2012.

Noah Webster, 1833

OCTOBER 16, 1847: *Jane Eyre An Autobiography* was published; it was "edited by Currer Bell," aka Charlotte Bronte, the author.

In 2013, a three-volume first edition sold for $57,461 at Bonhams.

Charlotte Bronte

OCTOBER 16, 1923: Walt and Roy created the Disney Brothers Cartoon Studio. Disneyland opened in 1955, and Disney collectibles abound.

In 1999, a cel from the first Mickey Mouse cartoon in color, *The Band Concert* (1935), changed hands in a private sale for $420,000 (www.animationvalley.co.uk).

The Band Concert (Photo courtesy of Heritage Auctions, HA.com)

In 2011, the same cel topped out at $44,812.50. Heritage Auction noted in the description that this cel had sold more than once for six figures.

OCTOBER 17, 1918: Birthday of actress and top World War II pin-up girl Rita Hayworth (born Margarita Carmen Cansino). With sixty-five film credits during her career spanning 1934 to 1972, she was a screen idol of the 1940s.

A two-piece outfit from her movie *Gilda* (a cream-colored crop top with a cutaway back and a wrap skirt) sold for $161,000 in 2014 at Bonhams. Her pin-up photo from *You'll Never Get Rich* (1941) sold for $84 in 2012, but a *Gilda* movie poster Style B one sheet (27.5 x 41 inches),

Rita Hayworth, 1947

(Continued on the next page.)

professionally restored, zoomed to $77,675 in 2014, both at Heritage Auctions.

This 1959 reissue of the 1946 *Gilda* blue dress poster sold for $956 at Heritage Auctions. (*Photo courtesy of Heritage Auctions*)

OCTOBER 18, 1939: The birth of Lee Harvey Oswald. A letter written to his mother from the Soviet Union sold for $51,520 in 2016 at Goldin Auctions.

OCTOBER 18, 1969: *The Nativity with St. Francis and St. Lawrence,* or *The Adoration,* painted by Caravaggio in 1609 was stolen from the Oratory of San Lorenzo in Palermo, Sicily. Valued at $20 million (art-crime.blogspot.com, 2009), the six-meter-square masterpiece has not been recovered, but it has been recreated by scanning a small photograph of it. The reproduction was returned to the Oratory.

The Nativity

OCTOBER 19, 2014: Ian McKellen's "Gandalf The White" screen-used hero Wizard's Staff from *The Lord of the Rings* Trilogy conjured up $390,000 at Profiles in History.

OCTOBER 19, 1216: King John of England died this day, the year after he signed the Magna Carta. While it has been hailed as a great document of liberty, it did not resolve the conflict between King John and the rebel barons. It was mostly ignored by both sides.

King John's tomb in Worchester Cathedral in Worchester, England

[Continued on the next page.]

A 1215 Magna Carta in the British Library

In 2007, Sotheby's auctioned for $21,321,000 one of the seventeen remaining Magna Cartas copied in 1297. Four originals from 1215 still exist.

An illuminated manuscript from c. 1300–1400 of King John on a stag hunt with hounds

OCTOBER 20, 1931: Baseball great Mickey Mantle was born. A 1952 Topps Mickey Mantle #311 PSA NM-MT 8 homered for $525,800 in 2015 at Heritage Auctions.

In addition to being one of the greatest ballplayers of all time, he was also a great person. These words of his reflect why:

"After I hit a home run, I had a habit of running the bases with my head down. I figured the pitcher already felt bad enough without me showing him up rounding the bases."

"Heroes are people who are all good with no bad in them. That's the way I always saw Joe DiMaggio. He was beyond question one of the greatest players of the century."

"As far as I'm concerned, Aaron is the best ball player of my era. He is to baseball of the last fifteen years what Joe DiMaggio was before him. He's never received the credit he's due."

"Roger Maris was as good a man and as good a ballplayer as there ever was." (All from brainyquote.com)

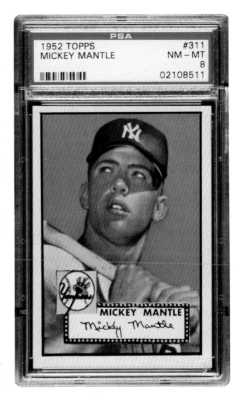

(Photo courtesy of Heritage Auctions)

OCTOBER 21, 1956: Carrie Frances Fisher, the daughter of Debbie Reynolds and Eddie Fisher, was born. She will always be remembered as Princess Leia, and her Slave Leia costume worn in *Star Wars: Episode VI—Return of the Jedi* will not be forgotten. It brought $96,000 at Profiles in History in 2015.

Her strangling of Jabba the Hutt with her slave chain won't be forgotten, either.

Carrie Fisher (Photo courtesy of Riccardo Ghilardi)

The Slave Leia costume (Photo courtesy of Profiles in History)

OCTOBER 22, 1938: Christopher Lloyd appeared for the first time. His first movie role was as Max in *One Flew Over The Cuckoo's Nest*. A star on film and TV, Lloyd has won three Primetime Emmys (IMDb.com). Of course, he will never be forgotten as Doc Brown in the *Back to the Future* movies.

In 2011, Profiles in History sold the time-traveling DeLorean used in the third movie for $541,200 with the proceeds benefitting the Michael J. Fox Foundation for Parkinson's Research. In all, seven DeLoreans were made for the movies; three remain in this timeline.

Christopher Lloyd, 2015 (*Photo courtesy of Gage Skidmore*)

OCTOBER 22, 2014: An Apple-1 motherboard, power supply, keyboard, and monitor powered to a record price of $905,000 at Bonhams. Others have sold for less. In 2010, an Apple-1 motherboard sold for $212,267 at Christie's, and in 2012, one auctioned at Sotheby's for $374,500.

This $905,000 motherboard is from the batch of the first

An Apple 1 motherboard (*Photo courtesy of Binarysequence*)

fifty Apple-1 computers built by Steve Wozniak and sold by Steve Jobs and Wozniak to the Byte Shop. The shop retailed them for $666.66 each. The first owner recognized its historical importance and safely stored it away in 1989. It came with only four kilobytes of memory that could be expanded to eight or forty-eight kb with expansion cards.

OCTOBER 23, 1940: Edson Arantes do Nascimento, Pelé, was born and became a Brazilian soccer legend. His record of 1,281 goals scored in 1,363 games (including amateur and reserve games) still stands.

In June of 2016, his 2,000-item collection of memorabilia was a hit at Julien's Auctions with these scores: a Jules Rimet special replica trophy presented to Pelé for being the first player to win three World Cups, $567,360; and his 1962 and 1970 FIFA World Cup Winner's Medals, $202,752 and $498,240, respectively.

Pelé (*Photo courtesy of Fábio Rodrigues Pozzebom/Agência Brasil*)

OCTOBER 24, 1852: Senator Daniel Webster passed away, one of the great American orators. He was Secretary of State twice, and with Henry Clay, he tried to avert the Civil War with the Compromise of 1850.

Webster is portrayed in the short story, "The Devil and Daniel Webster" by Stephen Vincent Benét. In it, he defends a man on trial who has sold his soul to Old Scratch and wants it back. An 1852 daguerreotype of Daniel Webster, 2.25 x 2.5 inches, went for $2,375 at Heritage Auctions in 2015.

Daguerreotype of Daniel Webster
(*Photo courtesy of Heritage Auctions, HA.com*)

OCTOBER 25, 1881: Pablo Picasso was born to give life a new look. A painter, sculptor, ceramics maker, printmaker, and author, Picasso's *Les femmes d'Alger* (Version 'O') skyrocketed to $179,365,000 at Christie's in 2015, putting it at #7 in the top ten paintings ever sold to date. Not far behind, his *Garçon à la Pipe* (Boy with a Pipe) spiked at $104,168,000 in 2004 at Sotheby's. It is currently #16 on the list.

Picasso's *Garçon à la Pipe*, 1905

OCTOBER 25, 1993: A great voice fell silent this day with the passing of Vincent Price. An extraordinary actor also, he brought chills in *The Fly*, *House of Usher*, and *The House on Haunted Hill*. Price's distinctive voice can be heard in Michael Jackson's *Thriller* and laughing manically at the end. He also voiced "Professor Ratigan" in *The Great Mouse Detective*.

A collector of art, Vincent Price and his wife Mary Grant donated ninety works to the East Los Angeles

Vincent Price in *The Bat*

House on Haunted Hill poster (*Photo courtesy of Heritage Auctions, HA.com*)

College in 1957, which then created the Vincent Price Art Museum in his honor (vincentpriceartmuseum.org).

In 2007, an Australian three sheet *House on Haunted Hill* (1959) poster, 41 x 81 inches, brought $507 at Heritage Auctions.

OCTOBER 26, 1881: Wyatt, Virgil, and Morgan Earp, and Doc Holliday rendezvoused with Ike and Billy Clanton, Billy Claiborne, and Tom and Frank Mc-Laury at the O.K. Corral—well, close by—for the most famous gunfight in history. The Earps went to disarm the Clanton gang, but when the smoke cleared, Billy Clanton and Tom and Frank were dead. Virgil, Morgan, and Doc were wounded.

A Colt .45-caliber revolver owned by Wyatt Earp sold for $225,000 at J. Levine Auction in 2014.

Wyatt Earp

Wyatt Earp's Colt (*Photo courtesy of J. Levine Auction and Josh Skalniak*)

OCTOBER 27, 1858: Theodore "Teddy" Roosevelt was born. He was the 26th President of the United States, from 1901 to 1909. Yes, the Teddy bear was named after him, due to a smart marketing ploy. After the President refused to shoot an old bear that hunting guides had tied to a tree for him, the story went out, and candy shop owner Morris Michtom began selling stuffed bears he called "Teddy bears" (theodoreroosevelt.org).

The highest price paid for a Teddy bear was $2.1 million in a charity auction in Monaco in 2000 for a Steiff bear with a designer coat and hat and a Louis Vuitton suitcase (justcollecting.com). In 2010, James D. Julia Auctions sold President Roosevelt's F-Grade A.H. Fox 12-gauge shotgun used on his 1909 African safari for $862,500.

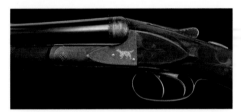

Theodore Roosevelt, 1903

Roosevelt's Fox shotgun (*Photos courtesy of James D. Julia Auctioneers, Fairfield, ME, www.jamesdjulia.com*)

OCTOBER 28, 1886: The Statue of Liberty was dedicated this day. This gift from the people of France is 151 feet, one inch in height and has outer copper sheeting which has oxidized to give it the iconic green color. It is a representation of the Roman goddess Libertas holding a book with "July 4, 1776" engraved on it. The Statue of

Frédéric Auguste Bartholdi

The head of the Statue of Liberty on display in a park in Paris in 1883

Liberty was designed by Frédéric Auguste Bartholdi and constructed by Gustave Eiffel, of Eiffel Tower fame.

The Statue of Liberty was sold a few years ago—at least, some of the inner metal and brick scraps from its renovation in the 1980s were sold (wsj.com, 2/24/14). In 2012, an Andy Warhol *Statue of Liberty* silkscreen canvas showing the statue repeated twenty-four times and colored in green and red, measuring 77.75 x 81 inches, auctioned for $43,762,500 at Christie's.

Gustave Eiffel

OCTOBER 29, 1929: Black Tuesday, 16 million shares were traded on the Stock Exchange, the most to date, confirming the Wall Street Crash that started on October 24.

A late-19th to early 20th century street sign from the intersection of Wall Street and Broad Street sold for $116,000 at Christie's in 2010. The sign was originally located near the New York Stock Exchange and the former headquarters of J.P.

(Continued on the next page.)

Morgan & Company and was pockmarked from the Wall Street Bombing on September 16, 1920. Terrorists detonated a wagon loaded with one hundred lbs. of dynamite and hundreds of pounds of iron weights at lunch time, killing thirty-eight people and injuring hundreds (history.com, 9/14/15). The perpetrators were never captured.

The Wall Street Bombing, 1920

OCTOBER 30, 1938: The night America was invaded by Martians, thanks to Orson Welles. His radio adaptation of H.G. Wells' *War of the Worlds* is not believed to have caused nationwide panic—as many think—since few heard the broadcast. The media, however, sold it as causing terror. What it did cause was instant notoriety for Orson Welles.

Orson Welles with the media the next day

His *War of the Worlds* radio show transcript sold for $28,800 at Profiles in History in 2015.

OCTOBER 31, 1632: The baptism of master artist Johannes Vermeer. He produced masterpieces, but relatively few over his lifetime. His world-famous *Girl with a Pearl Earring* resides in the Mauritshuis Art Museum in The Hague. The work is not a portrait.

Vermeer's *A Young Woman Seated at the Virginal* (a keyboard instrument) auctioned for $30,140,259 at Sotheby's in 2013 (news.artnet.com, 8/19/13). For many years, it was doubted that Vermeer was the painter of it, but after a decade of research, it was determined to be his work.

Girl with a Pearl Earring

A Young Woman Seated at the Virginal

The Concert

Johannes Vermeer

NOVEMBER

NOVEMBER 1, 1800: President John Adams moved into the completed White House. Costing nearly a quarter of a million dollars, President Adams wrote to his wife Abigail saying, "Before I end my letter, I pray Heaven to bestow the best of Blessings on this House and all that shall hereafter inhabit it. May none but honest and wise Men ever rule under this roof" (whitehouse.gov).

The earliest known photo of the White House, 1846

In 2012, two Kennedy Administration Cabinet Room chairs, accompanied by an autographed letter of presentation signed by Jacqueline Kennedy, realized $146,500 in 2012 at Sotheby's. They were given to Secretary of Defense Robert McNamara by the First Lady after her husband's death. McNamara's widow reported her husband referred to the Chippendale-style mahogany armchairs as "the President's."

NOVEMBER 2, 1755: Birthday cake today for Marie Antoinette who married, at the age of fourteen, the future King Louis XVI of France. Both were guillotined for treason in 1793.

A Royal Louis XVI giltwood enclosed armchair belonging to Marie Antoinette was auctioned at Christie's in 2015 for $2,714,250.

"Let them eat cake" has never been confirmed to have crossed her lips.

Marie Antoinette, 1775

NOVEMBER 3, 1948: "Dewey Defeats Truman," reported the *Chicago Tribune*, probably the most famous headline ever printed because it was incorrect. According to deweydefeatstruman.com, prices for this edition are affected by condition, completeness (that edition had three sections), and authenticity.

DEWEY DEFEATS TRUMAN

(*Photo courtesy of deweydefeatstruman.com*)

Those in very good condition average $2,000–$3,500 (auction vs. retail and if professionally framed). The highest paid on the website was $7,500 for an edition signed by Harry Truman. For an unsigned, framed, complete paper in superb condition, the highest was $3,500. Originals in poor condition with just the front page can be found for under $1,000. The front page alone has some value. This newspaper originally sold for four cents.

NOVEMBER 4, 1862: Dr. Richard Gatling's rapid-fire weapon, the Gatling gun, was patented.

The highest amount paid to date was $395,000 in 2014 at Heritage Auctions for a Colt Model 1877 Bulldog Gatling gun, .45-.70 caliber with five 18-inch barrels.

Teddy Roosevelt wrote that the use of Gatling guns saved the day in the charge up Kettle Hill (which is beside San Juan Hill) of his unmounted Rough Riders. (Only he was mounted to ensure his men saw him; also,

The Bulldog Gatling gun (*Photo courtesy of Heritage Auctions, HA.com*)

they supported Buffalo Soldiers who were in the main charge.) In 2001, Theodore Roosevelt posthumously received the Medal of Honor for his actions there.

NOVEMBER 4, 2008: The author Michael Crichton passed away from lymphoma. Overachievers take note: in addition to writing more than thirty novels and nonfiction books (*Jurassic Park, The Lost World,* and *The Andromeda Strain*), being a screenwriter (*Westworld, Coma, Jurassic* Park) and creator/writer/producer on TV's *ER,* he also earned his M.D. from Harvard Medical School.

Michael Crichton (*Photo courtesy of Jon Chase/ Harvard News Office*)

In addition, Crichton was an outstanding collector of art. In 2010, Christie's sold thirty-one pieces from his collection for $93,323,500 including: Jasper Johns' *Flag,* $28,642,500; Pablo Picasso's *Femme et fillettes,* $6,578,500; Roy Lichtenstein's *Figures in Landscape,* $4,338,500; and Jeff Koons' *Vase of Flowers,* $2,322,500.

NOVEMBER 5, 1913: English actress Vivien Leigh was born in Darjeeling, India. She won Best Actress Academy Awards for *Gone With The Wind* and *A Streetcar Named Desire* (IMDb. com). The straw hat she wore in several scenes in *GWTW* sold for $52,500 at Heritage Auctions in 2015.

Vivien Leigh

Scarlett's straw hat (*Photo courtesy of Heritage Auctions, HA.com*)

NOVEMBER 5, 2015: Andy Warhol's four colorful silkscreen prints of Muhammad Ali sold for $112,500 at Rago Arts & Auction, and a silkscreenprint of Grace Kelly made $106,250 at the same sale.

Muhammad Ali

NOVEMBER 6, 1946: Berta Hummel, later known as Sister Maria Innocentia Hummel, passed away. As a nun in Germany, she taught at an art school and created paintings of children. Some of these were reproduced as postcards and later in a book. Impressed with her work, porcelain manufacturer Franz Goebel began producing Hummel figures.

Most of these collectibles sell for only tens of dollars, and relatively few sell in the hundreds—which means Hummels are economical to collect. Only the very rare are higher in price, such as an early Goebel Hummel Flower Madonna auctioned for $1,565 on eBay in 2016.

Flower Madonna (*Photo courtesy of eBay seller gunnerhood*)

NOVEMBER 7, 2015: John Lennon's original 1962 J-160E Gibson Acoustic guitar, called the most important Beatles guitar to be auctioned, skyrocketed to $2,410,000 at Julien's. With Lennon playing it, the Beatles recorded, "She Loves You," "I Want to Hold Your Hand," "Please, Please, Me," "All My Loving," and many other hits. It was purchased in 1962 and lost in 1963 when a member of the road crew left it behind at a concert. It turned up in a San Diego guitar shop and changed hands twice before the auction (guitarworld.com, 11/10/15).

NOVEMBER 8, 1847: Author of a dozen novels—including *Dracula*—Bram Stoker was born in Ireland. His other job was as an actor's agent.

Before today's zombie craze, Count Dracula was the master of the undead. An 1897 signed

Bram Stoker

(Photo courtesy of Heritage Auctions, HA.com)

first edition of *Dracula* sold for $33,460 in 2006. A 1931 *Dracula* one sheet Style F movie poster, from the collection of Nicolas Cage, hit the record books at $310,700 in 2009. Both sold at Heritage Auctions.

NOVEMBER 8, 1900: Margaret Mitchell was born, which caused a straw hat to sell for $52,500.

NOVEMBER 8, 1960: John F. Kennedy was elected President of the United States, the 35th.

His leather bomber jacket with a sewn patch of the Great Seal of the President sold for $655,500 at John McInnis Auction. The sale also included a signed thank-you letter from Ronald Reagan for the loan of the jacket and photographs of J.F.K. wearing the jacket.

NOVEMBER 8, 1978: A part of America died this day with the passing of Norman Rockwell. He recorded poignant and humorous moments of American life, such as *The Gossips*, which sold for $8,453,000 at Sotheby's in 2013. In the painting, Rockwell portrayed fifteen sets of figures (his actual neighbors) passing gossip that circled back to its originator. *The Gossips* was the cover photo for the March 6, 1948 issue of the *Saturday Evening Post*.

Norman Rockwell

NOVEMBER 9, 1989: The Berlin Wall came down politically as East and West Germans were allowed to cross the barrier. In the ensuing days, the wall began to be physically taken down. Chips and blocks of it were taken by souvenir hunters, and many pieces sold for quite a few dollars. Today, pieces of the symbol of the end of the Cold War can be purchased for just a few dollars. It extended for ninety-six miles around Berlin so there are lots of pieces to sell.

NOVEMBER 10, 1958: The Hope Diamond was donated by Harry Winston to the Smithsonian—by sending it through the mail. The 45.52-carat blue diamond was shipped by registered first class mail for $2.44—with $1 million in insurance at a cost of $142.85 (USPS.gov/who-we-are).

The package that carried the Hope Diamond

The Hope Diamond (*Photo courtesy of David Bjorgen*)

NOVEMBER 11, 1620: The Mayflower Compact was signed by forty-one men aboard the *Mayflower* for the governing of the people who would be known as the Pilgrims of Plymouth Colony. It read in part: ". . . by virtue hereof to enact, constitute, and frame, such just and equal laws, ordinances, acts, constitutions, and offices, from time to time, as shall be thought most meet and convenient for the general good of the colony; unto which we promise all due submission and obedience."

John Alden was the seventh signer of it, and a document dated January 23, 1663 and signed by him sold in 2009 for $15,535 at Heritage Auctions. Alden married Priscilla Mullens who was made famous in the poem, *The Courtship of Miles Standish*, by Henry Wadsworth Longfellow.

The document signed by John Alden
(Photo courtesy of Heritage Auctions, HA.com)

NOVEMBER 12, 1929: The birthday of Grace Kelly, actress and Princess of Monaco. She won an Academy Award (not for *Rear Window*, but for *The Country Girl*) and three Golden Globes (IMDb.com). Alfred Hitchcock cast her in three movies: *Dial M for Murder* (1954); *Rear Window* (1954); and *To Catch a Thief* (1955).

A Christian Dior gown worn by Grace Kelly was auctioned for $72,000 at Julien's in 2012. A *Rear Window* one sheet sold for $9,560 in 2013 at Heritage Auctions.

Grace Kelly

Rear Window poster (*Photo courtesy of Heritage Auctions, HA.com*)

NOVEMBER 12, 2013: Jeff Koons' *Balloon Dog* (Orange), 1994–2000, sold at Christie's for $58,405,000—the highest price paid for a work of art by a living artist (nyt.com, 11/12/13). Made of mirror-polished stainless steel with transparent color coating and measuring 121 x 143 x 45 inches, the artwork was signed and dated, "Jeff

Balloon Dog (Orange) (*Photo courtesy of and © Jeff Koons*)

Koons 1994–2000." *Balloon Dog* was also produced in blue, magenta, red, and yellow versions.

NOVEMBER 12, 2013: A signed Andy Warhol black-and-white painting portraying a Coke bottle with most of the words "Coca-Cola" (the "la" was cut off "Cola") and titled, *Coca-Cola [3]*, popped to $57,285,000 at Christie's in 2013.

Warhol said: "What's great about this country is that America started the tradition where the richest consumers buy essentially the same things as the poorest. You can be watching TV and see Coca Cola, and you know that the President drinks Coca Cola, Liz Taylor drinks Coca Cola, and just think, you can drink Coca Cola, too. A coke is a coke and no amount of money can get you a better coke than the one the bum on the corner is drinking. All the cokes are the same and all the cokes are good. Liz Taylor knows it, the President knows it, the bum knows it, and you know it."

NOVEMBER 13, 1850: Birthday of Robert Louis Stevenson in Edinburgh, Scotland. He was the author of *The Strange Case of Dr. Jekyll and Mr. Hyde*, *Treasure Island*, *Kidnapped*, and many more novels.

In 2010, an autographed two-page letter from him dated July 12, 1892, framed with an engraved portrait of the author, sold for $3,550 at Christie's.

Robert Louis
Stevenson

NOVEMBER 13, 1903: French master painter Camille Pissarro passed away at the age of seventy-three. His *Le Boulevard Montmartre, Matinée de Printemps* ran bids up to $32,108,062 at Sotheby's in 2014, an auction record for the artist. Pissarro, who most often painted rural scenes and people, created a series of paintings of this boulevard in Paris, and today, some of them are in the

Camille Pissarro

(Continued on the next page.)

Hermitage, the Metropolitan Museum of Art, the National Gallery of Victoria (Australia), and The Hammer Museum in Los Angeles.

Le Boulevard Montmartre, Matinée de Printemps

NOVEMBER 14, 1851: *Moby Dick* was published for the first time in the US. Herman Melville's tale of the White Whale and Captain Ahab continues to capture the imagination, particularly on film beginning with *Moby Dick* in 1956, starring Gregory Peck and several remakes since.

A first American edition of the book *Moby Dick* sold for $40,000, and even a fourth edition made $7,168 in 2014 at Swann Auction Galleries.

Herman Melville

NOVEMBER 14, 2007: A single Inverted Jenny stamp soared to $977,500 at Robert Siegel Auctions. A block of four of the famous 1918 misprints topped $4.8 million in 2014 (kovels.com, 11/4/14). In May 2016, a single Inverted Jenny graded XF-Superb 95 sold for $1,351,250 at Robert Siegel Auctions.

In 2006 and 2007, stampwants.com ran a promotion to give away an Inverted Jenny in a drawing of those who registered on its website. True to their word, they did give one away in December 2007, valued at $400,000 at the time, and it was a successful promotion (prnewswire.com, 12/17/07). However, the website no longer exists.

In 2013, the United States Postal Service reissued the Inverted Jenny stamp in a $2 denomination. Then, it announced that in addition to the 2.2 million sheets of Inverted Jenny stamps, it would also print one hundred Non-Inverted Jenny stamps as souvenirs and distribute them randomly. In the end, only twenty sheets of the right-side-up plane stamp were sent to post offices. Then came the Inspector General of the Postal Service saying that creating it was wrong because it had intentionally created a rarity.

An Inverted Jenny stamp

In 2014, Robert Siegel Auctions sold a sheet of six of the Non-Inverted Jenny stamps for $45,000.

NOVEMBER 15, 1891: The Desert Fox Erwin Rommel was born; he died by suicide, poisoning at his own hand on October 14, 1944. He was given the choice of suicide or trial by the People's Court (which was certain death) and disgrace for his part in the July 20, 1944 attempted assassination of Hitler at the Wolf's Lair. With suicide, he was also offered a pension for his family and burial as a hero with no mention of his taking his own life.

Rommel (*Photo courtesy of Bundesarchiv, Bild 146-1973-012-43 / CC-BY-SA 3.0*)

The aftermath of the assassination attempt (*Photo courtesy of Bundesarchiv, Bild 146-1972-025-10 / CC-BY-SA 3.0*)

(Continued on the next page.)

In 2014, RR Auction sold an archive of more than ninety-four letters to and from Rommel, forty-four with his signature, for $120,693. In one: "January 8, 1940—I saw the Fuhrer today for the first time since New Year's. Maybe we'll go to the front soon. It would be very nice if we had something to do."

NOVEMBER 16, 1960: Clark Gable passed away at the age of fifty-nine due to complications after a heart attack. Gable served in World War II as leader of a motion picture filming unit and as an observer/gunner on five combat missions in the Army Air Corps, one over Germany. Flak shot out an engine on one plane and went through his boot on another flight. He received the Air Medal and Distinguished Flying Cross during his tour.

His leather Army Air Corps flight jacket with a name tag stamped "Clark Gable" and a 303rd Bomb Group Association circular unit insignia patch hit $14,351 at Nate D. Sanders Auction in 2012.

Clark Gable

Gable's Air Corps jacket (*Photo courtesy of Nate D. Sanders Auction*)

NOVEMBER 17, 1917: The day the great sculptor Auguste Rodin passed away. He created *The Thinker, The Kiss, The Gates of Hell, The Burghers of Calais,* and other works.

The Thinker

The Burghers of Calais

Rodin

In the Hundred Years' War, King Edward III of England ordered the people of Calais to be executed unless six leading citizens offered themselves in their place. Six did so and would have been killed, but Edward's wife Queen Philippa secured their pardon.

The *Burghers of Calais* statue honors their courage.

Rodin's statue, *Eve après le Péché* (*Eve after the Sin*), signed and created in white marble, yielded $4,484,558 at Christie's in 2013.

NOVEMBER 18, 1928:

Steamboat Willie, the first synchronized sound Mickey Mouse cartoon (also featuring Minnie Mouse) premiered. For trivia buffs, *Plane Crazy* was the first Mickey Mouse cartoon.

(Continued on the next page.)

The *Steamboat Willie* drawing (*Photo courtesy of Heritage Auctions, HA.com*)

In 2015, an original twelve-field, two-peghole animation drawing from *Steamboat Willie* featuring Mickey and Pete sold for $7,767, and in 2008, a *Steamboat Willie* original art background showing a dock auctioned for $26,290, both at Heritage Auctions.

The dock background (*Photo courtesy of Heritage Auctions, HA.com*)

NOVEMBER 18: Hi-De-Ho jazz great and bandleader "Cab" Calloway passed away in 1994. He was born on Christmas Day in 1907.

Also this day, *Calvin and Hobbes* debuted in 1985. Bill Watterson's famous boy-and-toy-tiger comic strip was put to bed in 1995.

A Bill Watterson *Calvin and Hobbes* hand-colored Sunday comic strip original art dated 10-19-1986 sold for—hold onto your stuffed tiger—$203,150. But wait, there's more. A Bill Watterson *Calvin and Hobbes* 1989-90 calendar cover watercolor illustration original art (c. 1988) of Calvin and Hobbes asleep under their tree jumped to $107,550. Both sold in 2012 at Heritage Auctions.

Cab Calloway

NOVEMBER 19, 1863: President Abraham Lincoln gave the *Gettysburg Address* a few months after Union forces defeated the Confederate Army at Gettysburg, Pennsylvania, the turning point of the Civil War.

Abraham Lincoln's glasses
(*Photo courtesy of Nate D. Sanders Auctions*)

Hancock at Gettysburg by Thure de Thulstrup, showing Pickett's Charge, print by L. Prang & Co.

Abraham Lincoln's glasses were sold by Nate D. Sanders Auctions for $84,422 in 2013.

NOVEMBER 20, 1992: Windsor Castle caught fire due to a lamp being left against a curtain (independent.co.uk, 12/4/92). Several of the rooms were being refurbished at the time, and their contents had been removed. Some ceilings collapsed, and one hudred rooms were damaged, particularly the Queen's Private

An 1848 drawing of the Private Chapel

Chapel (where it started), the Crimson Drawing Room, and the Green Drawing Room. Considered a national disaster, the fire had a bright side in that the cost to repair the damage, £36.5 million, was partially funded by Buckingham Palace being opened for tours.

NOVEMBER 21, 1920: The birth of baseball legend Stan Musial in Donora, Pennsylvania. He was an All-Star twenty-four times and played in the 1942, 1944, and 1946 World Series. His batting average was .331 with 475 home runs.

(Continued on the next page.)

Stan Musial

A 2011 St. Louis Cardinals World Championship ring presented to him in November 2013 hit $191,200 at Heritage Auctions. Stan passed away on January 19, 2013.

Stan's ring (*Photos courtesy of Heritage Auctions, HA.com*)

Side view of Stan's ring

NOVEMBER 21, 1942: Tweety Bird was hatched by Warner Brothers and appeared in *A Tale of Two Kitties.*

In 2014, a Kathrine Baumann Limited Edition Full Bead Yellow & Red Crystal Tweety Bird Minaudiere evening bag, 4 x 5 x 3 inches, sold for $937.50 at Heritage Auctions. (Other Kathrine Bauman purses have sold in the shapes of: a Diet Coke Can, $3,107; a Vintage Coca-Cola Bottle, $2,270.50; Miss Piggy, $1,195; and a Milk Bone Dog Treat, $3,585. All at Heritage Auctions in 2011.)

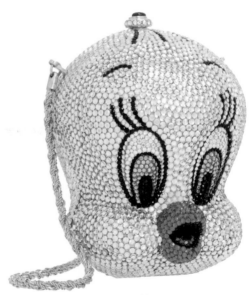

Tweety Bird bag
(*Photo courtesy of Heritage Auctions, HA.com*)

NOVEMBER 21-22, 2015: Heritage Auctions sold a treasure trove of seventeen movie posters and window cards found under a linoleum floor in a house being restored in York County, Pennsylvania, for $219,000. A few of those found were: an Italian two-foglio poster for *Casablanca*, $95,600; a window card for *Frankenstein*, $89,625; and a Style D one sheet poster for *Tarzan The Ape Man* for $83,650.

NOVEMBER 22, 1968: The Beatles' *White Album* (aka, *The Beatles*) was released featuring "Back in the USSR," "Ob-La-Di, Ob-La-Da," and "Helter Skelter." Ringo Starr's personal copy, estimated to sell for $60,000, hit $790,000 at Julien's in 2015—the second most valuable album in the world. The first? See November 24.

The white cover of the Beatles' *White Album*

NOVEMBER 22, 1963: Most people who were of age this day remember where they were—President John F. Kennedy was assassinated in Dallas, Texas.

The original keys to the 1961 Lincoln Model 74A limousine he and Jacqueline Kennedy were riding in sold for $26,290 at Goldin Auctions in 2016.

The President and his wife in the limousine

NOVEMBER 23, 1928:

The composer and lyricist for *Fiddler on the Roof,* Jerry Brock, was born. The movie won three Oscars from eight nominations. Brock won a Tony Award for Best Composer and Lyricist for the movie.

While *Fiddler on the Roof* movie posters sell for from a few dollars to a few hundred, a *Mad* magazine #156 *Fiddler on the Roof* cover illustration by Norman Mingo brought $8,962.50 in 2008 at Heritage Auctions. *Oye!*

Alfred E. Neuman as the Fiddler on the Roof (*Photo courtesy of Heritage Auctions, HA.com*)

NOVEMBER 24, 2014: Bert Lahr's Cowardly Lion costume from *The Wizard of Oz* sold for $3,077,000 at Bonhams.

The Cowardly Lion costume (*Photo courtesy of Bonhams*)

NOVEMBER 24, 2015: Rappers Wu-Tang Clan's *Once Upon a Time in Shaolin*, a 128-minute-long double album of thirty-one songs and stories, sold for reportedly $2 million (bloomberg.com, 12/9/12) in a private sale. Only one copy of the album was created to make it a work of art. As such, it was packaged in a hand-carved, nickel-silver box with a 174-page manuscript of the lyrics and information about the production of each song. The buyer was Martin Shkreli, the owner of Turing Pharmaceuticals (nyt.com, 9/20/15).

NOVEMBER 25, 1914: "Joltin' Joe" DiMaggio, the "Yankee Clipper," was born in Martinez, California. His fifty-six-game hitting streak in 1941 still stands today (baseball-almanac.com). Not getting number fifty-seven cost him $10,000 promised by Heinz 57 Sauce for an endorsement (newsday.com, 7/17/15). Nevertheless, he was a nine-time World Series champion, thirteen-time All-Star, American League MVP three times, AL batting champion, and home run leader twice. He died on March 8, 1999.

Joe DiMaggio

A 1942 New York Yankees Joe DiMaggio game-used and signed jersey hit $165,900 at Goldin Auctions in 2015 (psacard. com, 2/9/15).

NOVEMBER 26, 1922: Howard Carter entered the tomb of King Tutankhamun (or Tutankhamen or Tutankhamon) who died about 1323 BC. In addition to Tut's golden Death Mask, thousands of items were found, including in part: gold-overlaid furniture, coffins, and

[Continued on the next page.]

An alabaster jar found in King Tut's tomb (*Photo courtesy of Frank Rytell*)

The opening of the tomb's burial shrines

shrines; jeweled chests holding jewelry; model boats, six chariots; couches and chairs; two thrones; beds; statues; weapons; lamps; musical instruments; and 139 walking sticks of ebony, ivory, silver, and gold (historyembalmed.org).

NOVEMBER 27, 1940:

Bruce Lee was born, a master of martial arts. Known for *Enter the Dragon* and playing Kato in *The Green Hornet* TV series, his yellow jumpsuit with black stripes worn in the movie *Game of Death* sold for $100,500 at Spink in 2013 (cnn.com, 12/6/13).

Bruce Lee

Van Williams and Bruce Lee in *The Green Hornet*

Lee died at the age of thirty-two in 1973 of a cerebral edema. Yes, Bruce Lee was as fast as he seemed, and he was also a talented illustrator (hubpages.com/sports/Lost-Sketches-drawn-by-Bruce-Lee).

NOVEMBER 28, 1961:
Ernie Davis became the first African American to win the Heisman Trophy. He played for Syracuse and then was signed in the first round by the Cleveland Browns. He tragically passed away at the age of twenty-three to leukemia.

Davis' 1961 game-worn jersey made $33,460 in 2009, and his handwritten Heisman Trophy acceptance speech hit $11,352 in 2011, both at Heritage Auctions.

Ernie Davis' jersey
(*Photo courtesy of Heritage Auctions, HA.com*)

NOVEMBER 29, 1898: Clive Staples ("C.S.") Lewis was born. The author of *The Screwtape Letters*, the seven novels of *The Chronicles of Narnia*, and dozens of other books, an inscribed and signed copy of *The Lion, the Witch and the Wardrobe*, sold at Bloomsbury Auctions in London in 2012 for £36,600 (oxfordtimes.co.uk, 7/26/12).

C.S. Lewis

NOVEMBER 30, 1835: Birthday of Samuel Langhorne Clemens, America's Mark Twain. A hand-written draft chapter of his *A Tramp Abroad* gaveled for $79,300 at Leslie Hindman Auctioneers in 2010.

A book could be written about all the things Clemens/Twain said. Wait a minute, his quotes have filled about a dozen books. Just a few are:

"The lack of money is the root of all evil."

"Don't go around saying the world owes you a living. The world owes you nothing. It was here first."

"Get your facts first, then you can distort them as you please."

Samuel Clemens

NOVEMBER 30, 1874: Winston Leonard Spencer-Churchill was born at the right time for England.

An auction of his estate items reached £15,441,822 at Sotheby's in 2014. A skilled artist also, Churchill's painting, *The Goldfish Pool at Chartwell*, made £1.8 million in that sale (telegraph.co.uk, 12/17/14).

Winston Churchill
in uniform, 1895

DECEMBER

DECEMBER 1, 1984: Doug Flutie won the Heisman Trophy while playing at Boston College (brainyhistory.com). Flutie is most remembered for his 1984 Hail Mary touchdown pass of sixty-three yards with no time on the clock to beat the University of Miami, 47-45.

In 2006, his Heisman ring sold for $2,240.40 at Lelands Auction.

Doug Flutie's Heisman ring (*Photo courtesy of Lelands.com*)

DECEMBER 2, 1859: Painter Georges Seurat was born in Paris. He is known for originating the techniques known as pointillism and chromoluminarism, which is painting separate colors in dots so they combine like a full-color printing process. To paint this way was extremely time-consuming and difficult.

Some may not recognize his name, but most recognize Seurat's famous painting, *Island of the Grand Jatte* (1884); it auctioned at Sotheby's in 1999 for $35.2 million (cnn.com, 5/11/99).

Island of the Grand Jatte

Georges Seurat

DECEMBER 3, 2015: Ringo Starr's 1963 Ludwig Oyster Black Pearl drum kit used in 200 live performances and more than 180 studio recordings rocketed to $2,110,000 at Julien's Auctions.

Ringo Starr *(Photo courtesy of Eva Rinaldi)*

Ringo Starr's drum *(Photo courtesy of Julien's)*

DECEMBER 4, 2013: Norman Rockwell's *Saying Grace* sold at Sotheby's for $46,085,000—the highest paid to date for the artist. Measuring 43 x 41 inches, *Saying Grace* was his most popular cover painting for *The Saturday Evening Post*. It was featured on the cover on November 24, 1951.

Saying Grace
(Photo courtesy of Sotheby's)

DECEMBER 5, 2014: An 1891 Coca-Cola calendar sold at Morphy Auctions for $150,000. Two versions of it were printed; this one was the only known example of this variation.

1891 Coca-Cola calendar
(Photo courtesy of Morphy Auctions)

DECEMBER 5, 1901 AND DECEMBER 15, 1966: The birth and death dates of Walt Disney. Disney is the largest licensor of products in the world, and it all started in 1929 when Mickey Mouse's image was used on writing tablets for kids (disneyconsumerproducts.com).

A handwritten letter from Walt to Ub Iwerks dated to 1924 about his move to California sold for $247,800 at Profiles in History in 2011. Why so much? Iwerks worked with Disney in developing Mickey Mouse.

DECEMBER 5, 1870: The passing of Alexander Dumas, author of *The Count of Monte Cristo, The Three Musketeers, The Man in the Iron Mask,* and dozens of other novels. The popular *Count of Monte Cristo* has been seen on the big screen in more than one version as well as in comic books.

A carte de visite of Alexander Dumas sold in 2015 for $35 at Heritage Auctions.

The Alexander Dumas CDV
(Photo courtesy of Heritage Auctions, HA.com)

DECEMBER 5, 1791: Wolfgang Amadeus Mozart died at the age of thirty-five in Vienna, Austria.

A single-page note he wrote to a friend requesting the return of three scores of his music was sold for $217,000 by RR Auction in 2015. Mozart died penniless and was buried in a common grave.

Mozart,
c. 1780

DECEMBER 6, 1955: "Honus" Wagner passed away at the age of eighty-one. He was one of the first five players voted into the Baseball Hall of Fame, and he was so popular he tied with Babe Ruth in votes received (Ty Cobb received the most votes).

Playing for Pittsburg almost exclusively, Wagner's career batting average was .329 with 101 home runs and 722 stolen bases. He was the National League batting champion eight times, RBI leader five times, and stolen base leader five times.

In 2007, his T206 tobacco card, once owned by hockey great Wayne Gretzky, sold for $2.8 million.

A T206

DECEMBER 7, 2006: A .32 caliber Smith & Wesson engraved revolver presented to Major General John C. Fremont on April 14th, 1864 sold for $57,500 at Cowan's Auctions.

Fremont led five expeditions to explore and map the West, earning him the title of "The Pathfinder."

John C. Fremont

DECEMBER 8, 1980: John Lennon was shot in the back four times by Mark David Chapman who was seeking notoriety. Chapman received a twenty-year sentence and has been denied parole regularly.

A lock of John Lennon's hair trimmed for filming *How I Won the War* sold for $35,000. Also, his signed *Double Fantasy* album made $20,000, both at Heritage Auctions in 2016.

Double Fantasy album with John Lennon's signature and inscription across their faces (*Photo courtesy of Heritage Auctions, HA.com*)

DECEMBER 9, 2004: The Badminton Cabinet sold at Christie's for $36,662,106—the most expensive piece of furniture ever sold to date. Purchased by the Liechtenstein Museum in Vienna, Austria, this twelve-foot-tall cabinet made with ebony, gilt-bronze, and pietra dura, was originally commissioned in the early 1700s in Florence Italy, by nineteen-year-old Henry Somerset, the 3rd Duke of Beaufort. The cabinet received its title from the Earl's home, Badminton House in Badminton, Gloucester, England.

DECEMBER 10, 2010: General George Armstrong Custer's last flag from the Little Bighorn auctioned for $2,210,500 at Sotheby's. Discovered three days after the battle, it is known as the Culbertson Guidon because it was found by Sergeant Ferdinand Culbertson.

Also, an 1865 Model Spencer carbine owned by Custer sold at Heritage Auctions in 2012 for $179,250.

Custer's last flag (*Photo courtesy of Sotheby's*)

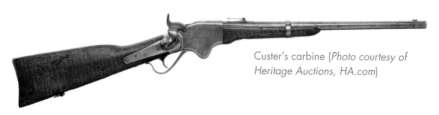

Custer's carbine (*Photo courtesy of Heritage Auctions, HA.com*)

DECEMBER 10, 2015: Janis Joplin's psychedelically painted 1964 Porsche 356 C 1600 SC Cabriolet roared to $1.76 million at RM Sotheby's. Joplin bought the car used.

The "Me and Bobby McGee" singer performed at Woodstock; she only released four albums before passing away at the age of twenty-seven.

Joplin's Porsche (*Photo courtesy of Sergio Calleja*)

Janis Joplin, 1970

DECEMBER 11, 1972: Apollo 17 landed on the moon, the last to do so.

Command Module pilot Ron Evan's OMEGA Speedmaster watch sold for $245,000 at Christie's in 2015. He remained in the module and did not walk on the moon; but he did walk in space during the mission while wearing the stainless steel watch.

The Apollo 17 crew

DECEMBER 12, 1915: Birthday cake for "Ol' Blue Eyes" Frank Sinatra. He won eleven Grammy Awards, and for *From Here to Eternity* (1953), he won an Oscar for Best Supporting Actor and a Golden Globe.

Sinatra was an avid collector of large toy trains (not model trains). In 2015, his little black book of addresses sold at Julien's Auctions for $8,960 (manoftheworld.com, 6-15-15).

On his grave marker is, "The Best Is Yet To Come." He died on May 14, 1998 (findagrave.com).

Frank in 1943

DECEMBER 13, 2012: Ralph DeLuca, owner of the movie collector website ralphdeluca.com, purchased a rare *Metropolis* (1927) movie poster in a lot with other classic posters for $1.2 million. Many versions were made of the *Metropolis* poster, but only four are known of this bronze-toned one that portrays the *Maschinenmensch* (machine-human) before the cityscape. Leonardo DiCaprio is said to own one, as does the Museum of Modern Art, and the Austrian National Library museum. In the lot were also posters from *King Kong*, *The Invisible Man*, and *Arsenic and Old Lace* (hollywoodreport.com, 12/13/12).

This restored *Metropolis* poster (*27 x 41 inches, Cinecom, R-1984*) showing the *Maschinenmensch* sold for $131.45 at Heritage Auctions (*Photo courtesy of Heritage Auctions, HA.com*)

DECEMBER 14, 1799: George Washington passed away at the age of sixty-seven. Exposure to rain and cold days before caused extreme throat soreness and finally dangerous difficulty in breathing. Doctors administered bloodletting in stages; up to half of his blood was taken. Yet, the exact cause of death has not been determined.

In 2012, George Washington's annotated copy of the Constitution and Bill of Rights (1789) sold for $9,826,500, and in 2009, a signed letter from 1787 to his nephew Bushrod Washington about the ratification of the Constitution hit $3,218,500, both at Christie's.

George Washington by Gilbert Stuart Williamstown

DECEMBER 15, 1890: Lakota Sioux war chief and holy man Sitting Bull was killed by Indian Agency policemen trying to arrest him, suspecting him to be part of an uprising. Several people were killed in the skirmish, including some of Sitting Bull's followers and policemen.

Sitting Bull participated in the battle against Custer at the Little Bighorn. Years later, he earned $50 per week performing with Buffalo Bill's Wild West Show, where he befriended Annie Oakley.

An original 4.25 x 6.5-inch cabinet card portrait of Sitting Bull sold for $29,005.20 at RR Auctions in 2012. It was imprinted on the front with photographer "Geo. W. Scott, Fort Yates, Dakota," and signed on the back "Sitting Bull." On the top it reads, "Autograph of Famous Sioux Indian War Chief Sitting Bull."

Sitting Bull's cabinet card with his signature on back (*Photos courtesy of RR Auctions*)

DECEMBER 16, 1775: *Pride and Prejudice* author Jane Austen was born.

In 2012, *American Idol* winner Kelly Clarkson bought her gold ring set with one round turquoise stone for $236,557 at Sotheby's in London but she was barred from taking it out of the country—it was deemed a national treasure. Jane Austen's House Museum—which is located in a house where Jane Austen lived and wrote—solicited donations and was able to purchase the ring from Clarkson (cnn.com, 9/24/15).

Jane Austen's ring (*Photo courtesy of Jane Austen's House Museum; photographer Peter Smith*)

DECEMBER 17, 1903: Orville Wright flew 120 feet lying on his stomach in the *Flyer I* at Kitty Hawk, N.C. His brother Wilbur actually flew on December 14th for about 112 feet, but the plane stalled so the four flights on the 17th are usually credited as their first powered

The Wright Brothers' first flight

flights. On the last flight of the day, Wilbur flew 852 feet in fifty-nine seconds (thewrightbrothers.org). Whether they were the first to fly in a powered machine is up for debate; others have been reported as doing so earlier.

A one-of-a-kind collection of diagrams drawn in pencil by Orville and Wilbur Wright, which included a drawing of a wing in profile showing lift properties and another of an overhead map of Kill Devil Hills where they made test flights, auctioned for $49,049.20 at RR Auctions in 2013.

DECEMBER 18, 1886: Birthday of Tyrus Raymond "Ty" Cobb in Narrows, Georgia. In 1909, "The Georgia Peach" took the AL's home run hitting title with just nine home runs—all inside the park (baseball-almanac.com, for 1909). His career batting average was .367 with 1,938 RBIs and 892 stolen bases.

Ty Cobb

The VG-EX + 4.5 T206 Ty Cobb card
(Photo courtesy of mintstateinc.com)

Cobb's record-making didn't end there. A family going through their great-grandparents' old house found a crumpled paper bag, and inside was another Cobb record—seven of his T206 White Border tobacco cards with "Ty Cobb King of the Smoking Tobacco World" on the back. Having one is rare; finding seven is a miracle.

Four of the so-named "Lucky Seven Find" have been sold privately to date for a total in excess of $1 million. The sales were brokered by Rick Snyder, President of MINT State Inc. The individual prices will not be revealed, but after all are sold, the final total will be. The cards were PSA graded 1.5 to 4.5, with 4.5 being the highest grade of this card (psacard.com/lucky7).

DECEMBER 18, 1966: *How The Grinch Stole Christmas* stole hearts big and small on this day, and it has been a Christmas tradition since.

A collection of twelve screen-used production cels from *How the Grinch Stole Christmas* sold for $90,000 at Profiles in History in 2015 (moviepropcollectors.com, 10/2/15).

DECEMBER 19, 1997: The blockbuster *Titanic* was released in the United States, and it won eleven Oscars and 109 other awards (IMDb.com). No Oscars for acting, though, for Leonardo DiCaprio or Kate Winslet. On a budget of $200 million, it made $2.2 billion worldwide (the-numbers.com).

Of course, artifacts from the real *Titanic* are always a hot collectible. The most paid to date was $1,454,400 for the violin that belonged to bandleader Wal-

Wallace Hartley and his violin (*Photo courtesy of mormonmusic.org*)

lace Hartley; it was found in a leather case attached to his body when he was recovered from the ocean (cnbc.com, 10/19/13). The violin was sold in 2013 by Henry Aldridge & Son. Kate Winslet's pink coat worn while sloshing around below decks to find Jack made $164,520 in February 2013 at Nate D. Sanders Auctions.

DECEMBER 20, 1957: Elvis Presley received his draft notice from the Army, and he willingly served. By this time, he was a star with hits like "Heartbreak Hotel," "Blue Suede Shoes," "Hound Dog," "Love Me Tender," All Shook Up," and "Jailhouse Rock." The Army granted him a deferment from reporting because he was in the middle of filming *King Creole*.

Elvis at his swearing in

Elvis' Army winter dress uniform sold for $46,875 at Julien's in 2015.

DECEMBER 21, 1911: Negro Leagues slugger Josh Gibson was born. Playing catcher for the Homestead Grays of Pennsylvania, his career batting average was .359 (possibly higher since Negro Leagues' records are not complete) with a .648 slugging percentage (baseballhall.org). He was a Negro World Series champion twice and twelve times an All-Star. In barnstorming postseason play between Major League and Negro League teams, Gibson averaged .412. His best season saw him bat .517 and hit eighty-four home runs (mlb.mlb.com, "Negro Leagues").

Sometimes called "The Black Babe Ruth," he was inducted into the Baseball Hall of Fame in 1972, right after Satchel Paige. Gibson died early at the age of thirty-five from a stroke.

A twice-signed 1931 real photo postcard of Gibson, during his first full season, sold for $81,200 at Robert Edward Auctions in 2006.

Josh Gibson's photo postcard

The back of the card with an inscribed note and a second signature (*Photos courtesy of robertedwardauctions.com*)

DECEMBER 22, 1941: Archie Andrews first appeared in *Pep Comics #22* and has been a perpetual teenager since. He was drawn by Bob Montana and written by Vic Bloom. An *Archie Comics #1* (1942) CGC VF+ 8.5 brought $167,300 in 2011 at Heritage Auctions.

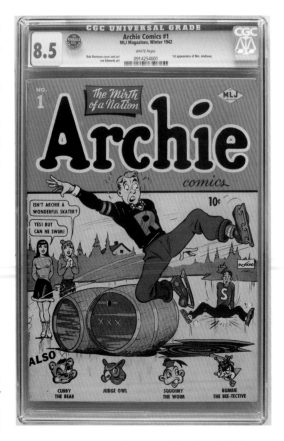

Archie at the top of his game (*Photo courtesy of Heritage Auctions, HA.com*)

DECEMBER 23: In 2000, the talented pianist and comedian Victor Borge passed away at ninety-one. One of his famous routines was to play a bunch of unharmonious notes, stop, turn his sheet music upside down, and then play the song correctly.

A pair of wire-rim glasses, owned and worn by John Lennon and presented to Borge, who provided piano backup for him, sold for $23,076.55 at RR Auction in 2014.

Victor Borge
(*Photo courtesy of Jesper Jurcenoks*)

DECEMBER 24, 1809: Hunter, trapper, frontiersman, guide, explorer, and hero of dime novels Christopher Houston "Kit" Carson was born.

His 1816 flintlock pistol issued for the Mexican-American War sold for $18,000 at Manitou Galleries in 2012.

Kit Carson's flintlock pistol (*Photo courtesy of Manitou Galleries*)

Kit Carson, c. 1868

DECEMBER 25, 1776: George Washington crossed the Delaware River and defeated Hessian troops in Trenton, N.J. German artist Emanuel Gottlieb Leutze (1816-1868) painted his idealized *Washington Crossing the Delaware* three times. The original was destroyed in Allied bombing in 1942; the second, begun in 1850, was purchased the next year by Marshall O. Roberts for $10,000 (Metmuseum.org). After being sold a few times, it was donated to the Metropolitan Museum of Art in 1897 where it resides today. The third is held by the Minnesota Marine Art Museum.

Emanuel Leutze

Washington Crossing the Delaware

DECEMBER 26, 1991: The snub-nosed .38 Colt Cobra Jack Ruby used to kill Lee Harvey Oswald sold for $220,000 in Las Vegas (baltimoresun.com, 12/27/91).

DECEMBER 27: On this day were born: astronomer Johannes Kepler, 1571, in Germany; scientist Louis Pasteur, 1822, in France; and actress Marlene Dietrich, 1901, in Germany. Mathematician, astronomer, and all-around Brainiac, Kepler is lauded for plotting the orbit of Mars and defining three laws of planetary motion.

A 1609 first edition of his *The New Astronomy* folio of writings and illustrations sold for $357,149 at Sotheby's in 2014.

Johannes Kepler

DECEMBER 28, 1922: Stanley Martin Lieber, now known as Stan Lee, was born, and he went on to create or co-create the Incredible Hulk, Spider-Man, X-Men, Daredevil, The Fantastic Four, and Doctor Strange.

Spider-Man's first appearance in the 1962 *Amazing Fantasy #15* hit a record $454,100 at Heritage Auctions in 2016. It was near-mint CGC 9.4 and had been in a safety deposit box for thirty-five years.

The Human Torch isn't doing so badly. He was introduced in *Marvel Comics #1* in 1939; a CGC VF/NM 9.0 copy with off-white pages burned up $207,050 in 2010 at Heritage Auctions.

The Human Torch has evolved since *Marvel Comics #1*. (*Photo courtesy of Heritage Auctions, HA.com*)

DECEMBER 29, 1906: Joseph Christian Leyendecker's New Year's Baby character appeared on the cover of the *Saturday Evening Post* for the first time in *Cleaning Up*. The oil-on-canvas painting, signed and inscribed, swept up $137,000 in 2014 at Heritage Auctions.

Along with Norman Rockwell, Leyendecker was a prolific painter for the *Post*, creating 321 covers over four decades, starting in 1899. His Baby appeared on the cover numerous times, including celebrating the end of World War I.

JC Leyendecker

Cleaning Up

DECEMBER 30, 1865: Rudyard Kipling was born in Bombay, India. The author of *The Jungle Book*, *Captains Courageous*, *Kim*, and the poem "Gunga Din," he said, "A woman's guess is much more accurate than a man's certainty" (brainyquote.com).

A family archive of letters, photos, and personal items, sold for a total of £38,000 at Ewbank Auction in 2014.

Rudyard Kipling

DECEMBER 31, 1869: Birthday of artist Henri Matisse who lived until November 3, 1954.

His style and use of color, often bright, has landed much of his work in museums across the world. Matisse's 1911 painting, *Les coucous, tapis bleu et rose* (The Cowslips, Blue and Rose Fabric) sold for $46,286,022 at Christie's in a sale of fashion designer Yves Saint Laurent's estate.

Henri Matisse

Woman with a Hat, a work by Matisse, in the San Francisco Museum of Modern Art.

DECEMBER 31, 1937: Another artist was born this day, Anthony Hopkins. While mostly known for his artistic work on the big screen, Hopkins does paint. Other famous painters include: Viggio Mortensen, Pierce Brosnan, Sylvester Stallone, Jane Seymour, Johnny Depp, Tony Curtis, Anthony Quinn, Jack Palance, Phyllis Diller, Richard Chamberlain, and Buddy Ebsen (uniqueart.blogspot.cz).

The *Financial Times* reported Sylvester Stallone's work sells for between $50,000 and $120,000 (ft. com, 10/25/13). Phyllis Diller's painting of Bob Hope

Anthony Hopkins (*Photo courtesy of Elena Torre*)

auctioned for $16,250, and her painting, *Spotlight,* of a round circle of light on stage curtains, sold for $10,625 at Julien's in 2013.

Phyllis Diller (*Photo courtesy of Allan Warren*)

INDEX

Anne Frank's Grimm's Fairy Tales, June 12
Annie Oakley's Parker Brothers shotgun, August 13
Anti-smoking campaign, January 11
Antoinette, Marie, January 21, November 2
Apollo 13, April 11
Apollo 17, December 11
Apple-1 motherboard, October 22
Aragon's sword, February 29
Archie Comics #1, December 22
Aries 1B Trans-Lunar Space Shuttle from *2001 A Space Odyssey*, July 26
Armstrong, Louis, August 4
Armstrong, Neil, July 20, August 5
Arness, James, June 3
Arnold, Benedict, June 14
Arnold Palmer's golf clubs, September 10
Arthur Conan Doyle's archive, May 22
Asimov, Isaac, January 2
Atari, June 11
Atocha, cross, September 6
Augusta National, March 17
Augustus Saint-Gaudens Double Eagle, July 30
Austen, Jane, December 16
Axe, John "Gilmi" Rhys Davies', September 2

B
Babe Ruth, January 25, February 6, March 18, July 12, and July 14,
    700th home run ball, July 14
    Jersey, August 16
    Letter, July 12
    Photo with Gary Cooper, May 7
Babe Zaharias' golf bag and clubs, September 27
Bach cantata, March 31
Bach, Johann Sebastian, March 31
Back to the Future
    DeLorean, October 22
    Marty's Nike Mags, July 3
Badger, January 22
Badminton Cabinet, December 9
Bal du moulin de la Galette, February 25
Ball, Lucille, August 6
Banana sticker, January 6
Barber Dime, January 7
Barrow, Clyde, Mar 23
Bart Simpson, April 1
Bastille key, February 22
Batman, January 12
Batmobile, January 12
Baum, L. Frank, May 15
B.B. King's guitar, September 16
Beanie Babies, September 3
"Beat It" jacket, Michael Jackson, May 21

Beatles,
    Double Fantasy album, December 8
    Guitar, November 7
    John Lennon, December 8
    Paul McCartney, March 15
    Ringo Starr, July 7, December 3
    White Album, November 22
    Wire-rim eyeglasses, December 23
Beatrix Potter's *Tale of Peter Rabbit*, September 4
Beaulieu, Priscilla Ann (Presley), May 1
Beethoven, Ludwig van, March 26
Beetle Bailey, September 4
Bell, Alexander Graham, March 2, March 7
Ben-Hur script, October 4
Benny, Jack, February 14
Bergman, Ingrid, August 29
Berlin Wall, November 9
Berra, Yogi, September 22
Berwick Discovery of Lost Movie Posters, March 23
Beverly Hillbillies truck, September 26
Bible, Gutenberg, February 3
Big Campbell's Soup Can with Can Opener (Vegetable), January 9
Bill Monroe's mandolin, September 13
Bill of Rights, December 14
Billy the Kid, June 25
Bird, Larry, August 18
Black Betsy, "Shoeless Joe" Jackson's bat, August 7
Bligh, Captain William, April 28
Blood, Thomas, May 9
Board game, Jumanji, July 22
Bogart, Humphrey, March 20, March 26
Bonanza, July 1
Book of Mormon, August 29
Books,
    A Tramp Abroad, November 30
    Annie Oakley of The Wild West, August 13
    Book of Mormon, August 29
    Brave New World, July 26
    Chitty-Chitty-Bang-Bang: The Magical Car, May 28
    Dracula, November 8
    Down and Out in Paris and London, June 25
    Frankenstein, August 30
    From the Earth to the Moon, February 8
    Gone With The Wind, August 16
    Grimm's Fairy Tales, June 12
    History of the Expedition under the Command of Captains Lewis and Clark, May 14
    How I Found Livingstone, May 10
    In Cold Blood, September 30
    Ivanhoe, September 21

Inverted Jenny stamp, November 14
Island of the Grand Jatte, December 2
Ivanhoe, September 21

J

Jack Dempsey Heavyweight Championship belt, June 24
Jack Johnson trophy, March 31
Jacket
    Clark Gable, November 16
    Han Solo, April 11
    Michael Jackson, May 21, June 25
Jackie Robinson
    1952 Topps card, January 31
    Baseball glove, July 23
Jackson, Michael, February 1, May 21, June 25, August 29
Jackson, "Shoeless Joe", July 16, August 7
James Dean's t-shirt, September 30
James, Jesse, April 3
Jane Eyre, October 16
Janis Joplin's Porsche, December 10
Jaws, June 20
Jennings, Waylon, June 15
Jerseys,
    Babe Ruth's, August 16
    Ernie Davis', November 28
    Hank Aaron's, February 5
    Joe DiMaggio's, November 25
    Johnny Unitas', May 7
    Larry Bird's, August 18
    Michael Jordan's, April 18
    Willie Mays', May 6
Jesse James' wanted poster, April 3
Jim the Wonder Dog, March 18
J.K. Rowling's chair, July 31
Joan of Arc, January 6
Joe Louis Soda Punch sign, May 13
Joel, Billy, March 15
John Lennon's hair, December 8
John Philip Sousa photo, October 1
John Wayne's hat and memorabilia, May 26
Johnny Carson Friars Club Roast program, May 29
Johnson, Jack, March 31
Johnson, Walter, January 25
Jones, Bobby, March 17
Jones, Caroline (Morticia Addams), August 3
Joplin, Janis, December 10
Jordan, Michael, February 17, April 18
Josh Gibson postcard, December 21
Julia Child's pans, August 15
Jumanji board game, July 21
Jumpsuits,

Bruce Lee's, November 27
Elvis', May 1

K

L

Matisse, Henri, December 31
Matt Dillon, June 3
Maxwell, James Clerk, June 13
Mayfield, Curtis, March 15
Mayflower Compact, November 11
Mays, Willie, May 6
McCall, "Crooked Nose Jack" May 27
McCartney, Paul, March 15
McDaniel, Hattie, June 10
McGwire, Mark, September 8
McKellen, Ian, October 19
McQueen, Steve, March 24, June 26
Medals,
     Ernest Shackleton's, January 5
     Martin Luther King's, July 11
     Medal of Honor, July 27
     Pelé's, October 23
     William Bligh's, April 28
Melville, Herman, November 14
Menu, *Titanic*, April 14
Mercury 7 astronauts, April 9
Merry-go-round, May 17
Metropolis, movie poster, December 13
Michael Jackson,
     "Beat It" jacket, May 21
     Glove, August 29
     Thriller jacket, June 25
Michelangelo, March 6, September 8
Mickey Mantle 1952 Topps #311, October 20
Mickey Mouse, January 13, October 16
Mickey Mouse Club production cels, October 3
Microphone, Johnny Carson, April 21
Miller, Arthur, February 10
Milne, A.A., October 14
Milton, John, August 20
Minuteman Oliver Buttrick's powder horn, April 19
Missionary Travels and Researches in South Africa, May 10
Mitchell, Margaret, May 3, August 16, November 8
Moby-Dick, November 14
Model T, October 1
Molar, John Lennon, August 29
Molly Brown loving cup, April 14
Mona Lisa, August 21
Monroe, Bill, September 13
Monroe, Marilyn, January 14, February 10, May 19, June 1, June 18, June 27
Moonraker, May 28
Moore, Clayton (The Lone Ranger), September 14
Moore, Clement C., July 15
Mork from Ork spacesuit, July 21
Morrison, Marion Michael (John Wayne), May 26

Phantom V Touring Limousine, Elvis Presley's 1963 Rolls-Royce, January 8
Phaser rifle, August 19
Philosophiae Naturalis Principia Mathematica by Sir Isaac Newton, January 4
Phoenix cape from *Cleopatra*, June 12
Photographs,
    Babe Zaharias, September 27
    Boston, as the Eagle and the Wild Goose See It, October 13
    Daniel Webster daguerreotype, October 24
    Frederick Douglass, February 20
    Great Chicago Fire, October 7
    Groucho Marx, October 2
    Jacqueline Bouvier Kennedy Onassis, July 28
    John Philip Sousa, October 1
    Lucille Ball, August 6
    Migrant Mother, October 11
    Moonrise, Hernandez, Mexico, February 20
    Rita Hayworth, October 17
    Robert Louis Stevenson, November 13
    "Shoeless Joe" Jackson, July 11
    Sitting Bull, December 15
    Tarzan, August 3
    Will Rogers, August 15
Phyfe, Duncan, August 16
Piano in *Casablanca*, August 29
Picasso, Pablo, April 25, October 25, November 4
Pieta sculpture, March 6
Pike, Zebulon, April 27
Pissarro, Camille, November 13
Pistols,
    Al Capone's, January 25
    Bat Masterson's, August 2
    Bonnie Parker's, May 23
    Buffalo Bill Cody's, February 26
    Clint Eastwood's, May 31
    Doc Holliday's, August 14
    Jack Ruby's, December 26
    John C. Fremont's, December 7
    Kit Carson's, December 24
    Lone Ranger's, September 14
    Matt Dillon's, June 3
    Michael Landon's, July 1
    Samuel Colt's, February 25
    Wild Bill Hickok's, May 27
    Wyatt Earp's, October 26
Plan 9 From Outer Space, October 10
Poe, Edgar Allan, October 7
Poems on Various Subjects, May 8
Pony Express envelope, April 3
Poor Richard's Almanac, April 16
Popeye, March 26

Y

Yankee Doodle Dandy suit, July 17
Yogi Berra,
  Catcher's mask, September 22
  MVP plaque, September 22
  Rookie card, September 22
Young, Brigham, August 29
Young, Cy, March 29
Yul Brynner's bracelet from *The Ten Commandments*, July 11
Yvonne de Carlo's black cape, September 13, 2016

Z

Zaharias, Mildred E. "Babe," September 27